Methods of Teaching
INFORMATION TECHNOLOGY

Methods of Teaching INFORMATION TECHNOLOGY

Dr. T. Shankar

CRESCENT PUBLISHING CORPORATION

Methods of Teaching Information Technology

First Published : 2016

ISBN 81-8342-068-0

Published by :

CRESCENT PUBLISHING CORPORATION

4806/24,Mathur Lane,
Ansari Road, Darya Ganj,
New Delhi-110002
Mob.: 9711991838, 9999021668
Ph.: 011-23244131
E-mail : crescentbook@gmail.com
Website : www.crescentpublishingcorp,weebly.com

Printed at :

Roshan Offset Printers

Delhi

Preface

Information technology is a broad subject concerned with technology and other aspects of managing and processing information, especially in large organizations. In particular, IT deals with the use of electronic computers and computer software to convert, store, protect, process, transmit, and retrieve information. In all most all countries, information technology is formally integrated into the school curriculum. With the arrival of the internet and the broadband connections to all schools, the application of IT knowledge, skills and understanding in all subjects became a reality. This change in emphasis has resulted in a change of name from Information Technology (IT) to Information and Communication Technology (ICT). ICT in education can be understood as the application of digital equipment to all aspects of teaching and learning. It is present in almost all schools and is of growing influence.

The methods and strategies of teaching information technology are comprehensively described in this book. It shows teachers how to create an environment in which information technology can effectively enhance education. It also attempts to evaluate the modern teaching practices and provides key suggestions to improve the quality of teaching IT. The contents of the book will be highly beneficial to policy-makers, teacher educators, researchers and student-teachers.

Dr. T. Shankar

Contents

1 Introduction

Information and Communication Technologies (ICTs) have been utilised by education ever since their inception, but they have been massively present in schools only since the early 1980s. Developed countries have applied them to K-12 education for a variety of reasons, most of which are still valid today, although in many cases they have remained unfulfilled expectations. Some of these reasoning are:

— *A new society requires new skills:* ICT increasingly pervade every aspect of life (work, learning, leisure, and health). Because ICT are the preeminent tools for information processing, new generations need to become competent in their use, should acquire the necessary skills, and therefore must have access to computers and networks during their school life. There is an equity issue in this argument related to the need to prioritise access to ICT resources to the more underserved population, which is being left behind on a digital divide.

— *Productivity enhancement:* Schools are information- and knowledge-handling institutions; therefore, ICT should be fundamental management tools on all levels of an educational system, from classrooms to ministries.

- *A quest for quality learning:* Schools should profoundly revise present teaching practices and resources to create more effective learning environments and improve life-long learning skills and habits in their students. ICT are versatile and powerful tools that can help in this purpose and should therefore be present in every classroom, library and teacher room. It must be said, however, that so far ICT have not provided any large-scale breakthrough in learning improvements. They are still promises with great potential.

In terms of learning, it has been argued that a few subjects are being intrinsically changed because of ICT. For example learning science is increasingly related to having access to scientific databases, with information-sharing over the network, and with the use of digital devices for data processing. Languag- and societal communications are being modified because of the presence of Internet (i.e. chats, e-mail, forums and digital newspapers) and of handheld devices with communication capabilities. Although several counter-arguments have emerged (i.e. lack of hard, replicable evidence of educational impact, unfulfilled expectations of revolutionary changes, need for long-term investment and high recurrent costs), we have seen an increased pressure for a more rapid infusion of ICT into education in recent years.

Developing countries have become anxious about the widening gap between their reality and the aggressive ICT policies of countries such as the United States, Canada, and some of the northern European countries. The last ten years have produced a vast amount of research in the field of ICT in education with mixed results. Many projects have embarked on large-scale efforts using differing approaches, and technology itself has evolved at a rapid pace with many new promises for education every year. At the same time, the literature contains many unsubstantiated claims about the revolutionary potential of ICT to improve the quality of education.

Some claims are now deferred to a near future when hardware will be presumably more affordable and software will become, at last, an effective learning tool. Perhaps the most important lesson from past initiatives is that a technology-centered policy, i.e. one that focuses primarily on deploying machines, software and Internet connections, will not produce meaningful results or the expected impact on students learning. Although machines and networks are a fundamental component in any ICT policy, to achieve effective gains in student's learning, improved teaching practices and more efficient management at all levels (classroom, school, district and nation), the focus should *reside on people and how to improve and develop their* skills and practices with the help of ICT.

In order to have long lasting effects, to be effectively infused into the schools' culture, and to be considered relevant by teachers and school administrators, an ICT policy should preferably not be designed in isolation. Rather, it should be part of a more comprehensive effort towards improving the equity and quality of an educational system. Also, educational initiatives ought to be coordinated through all possible administrative and operational levels in order to effectively send coherent messages to teachers, parents and administrators.

Roles of ICT in the School

ICT can and should play a variety of roles inside a school. Some of the more important ones are pedagogical, cultural, social, professional and administrative. ICT, if sensibly deployed and with carefully selected software, can positively affect many aspects of school life, from a healthy questioning of present teaching practices to a gradual improvement of the quality, scope and depth of the learning environment, as well as to provide a remarkable opportunity for teachers' development.

Pedagogical Tool Role

An important role of ICT inside a school is that of providing a new framework that can foster a revision and an improvement of teaching and learning practices. Though many positive results have been reported on a small scale, there has been no breakthrough in learning improvements because of ICT on a large, replicable scale. Nevertheless, teachers and students can take advantage of the growing availability of educational resources as software packages and Web pages.

Teachers will need curricula-related content and clear strategies and examples to effectively use these materials in the classroom. They will find that students can become highly motivated towards learning if technology makes up part of their classroom experience. Teachers can fruitfully use this positive attitude to explore new learning strategies in which students can be more actively involved in learning, as opposed to being simply passive information receivers. Collaborative, project-based and self-paced learning are just a few alternatives amply documented and particularly appropriate to use when ICT are present.

Primary and secondary students with special talents (i.e. mathematics, music or literature) will find a vast amount of digital tools and resources as well as groups of similarly inclined youngsters all over the world with whom to share and develop their talents. On the other hand, students with special needs will also find resources and tools for remedial or self-paced learning. This can have a particularly high impact on more deprived and culturally isolated schools where primary students have fewer information resources and learning opportunities.

However, it is important to emphasise that it is not the presence of technology in itself that will stimulate significant changes inside a school. Without teacher involvement, most students in primary levels in particular, but also in higher levels may not take advantage of all the available potential on their own. Teachers need to become active participants for effective ICT educational use, such as providing guidance, help and usage rules for the students. Teachers are needed to organise the learning spaces and to guide toward the achievement of significant learning objectives.

In developing countries, students often do not acquire sufficient mathematical skills, a basic understanding of scientific concepts or an adequate reading comprehension level during their school years. ICT provides tools and content to exercise these abilities, which will be needed to take advantage of the vast amount of content present in today's networks. Information processing skills to transform data (i.e. searching, selecting, synthesising and communicating information) into knowledge is rapidly becoming a basic requirement for the emergent information society. If ICT policies are closely related to the curriculum, teachers will more likely use them for learning practices in classrooms.

Therefore, curriculum designers should consider the inclusion of ICT as transversal themes, i.e. in all curricular sectors, and in the curriculum-specification guidelines that will be used by teachers. It is not advisable to have ICT as separate, isolated technical subjects or sectors in the curriculum (e.g. programming, software tools and hardware configurations), because in this atmosphere, teachers will tend to regard ICT as special subjects and may not integrate them in their normal practice. Rather, ICT should be included as teaching and learning resources, along with examples of how to use them in classrooms, in all sectors, and in this way, turning them, explicitly, into a tool for all teachers in all grades and subject areas.

Cultural, Social, and Professional Roles of ICT

The cultural, social and professional roles of ICT are exercised primarily through an effective use of the vast amount of information sources and services available today via Internet and CD-based content for the entire educational community: students, teachers, administrators and parents. Also, nowadays new equipment and low-cost portable keyboards with text -handling capacities are helping teachers around the world with their professional routines. A school connected to the Internet can foster communication at local (i.e. inside a community), national and international levels.

Educational projects that connect students and teachers from different countries might amplify the quality of the conversational spaces, may expand students' horizons by allowing them to know and interact with people from other cultures and can stimulate group work and social interaction. For teachers, networks provide a medium to establish fluent links among peers from schools worldwide. Teachers can benefit greatly from sharing their experiences, problems and queries with colleagues in same situations.

Of similar importance is the growing field of e-learning, with the availability of a large number of training courses for teachers delivered through the Internet, thus providing new means for professional development regardless of the teacher's workplace. Bandwidth and communication quality can become major constraints. A low bandwidth and/or poor quality communication infrastructure can restrict network usability to text -only e-mails, limited to a few times a week. This is a far cry from the potential benefits of e-learning and from participating in professional groups and learning circles using high bandwidth connections. This is particularly important for geographically and/or culturally isolated schools, which are common in rural and suburban areas.

With up-to-date communications technology in place, students and teachers in these settings may experience a reduction in their cultural isolation and a significant improvement in their learning resources. Again, this will be highly dependent on the quality of the telecommunications infrastructure and its cost.

Administrative Roles

ICT have important roles to play in making school administration less burdensome and more effectively integrated to the official information flow about students, curricula, teachers, budgets and activities through the educational system information pipelines. They are also a good means for informing community members (parents, politicians, and researchers) about educational news and policies. At the classroom level, teachers can more easily keep student's marks and their personal and academic records permanently up-to-date, as well as produce all required data for school administration and for parents, using preformatted documents.

Most importantly, teachers can maintain their subject content (lesson plans, exercises, evaluation) in digital format, making it easy to update, to share with other teachers and to enhance with time. In fact, the many ways tools such as a computer, a handheld device or a portable keyboard (and a network) can help a teacher in administrative tasks is one of the more convincing arguments to make to inexperienced teachers so they will accept training eagerly. This should be carefully considered during teacher-training planning because before pedagogical use in the classroom, many teachers may prefer to become familiarised first with the technology outside the classroom.

This can often be facilitated greatly by starting out with software applications or simple devices such as portable keyboards or handhelds that can be of immediate use. It is relatively easy to learn how to use these machines to store text in a portable keyboard, to construct spreadsheets, or to make use of word processing to record students' marks and records. At the school level, administrators will appreciate the use of spreadsheets, word processors, small databases and special accounting software to organise and store all relevant data. Internet can help link the school with the Ministry of Education offices to make the transfer of documents, new regulations and queries more efficient throughout the system.

It can also help in improving the flow of information to the community through web sites and with regular well-designed information sheets. At the educational system level, policy-makers may consider the introduction of ICT at all three levels (classroom, school, system) as a great opportunity to acquire and to distribute information through the system and from the general public to the classroom teacher. A coordinated effort can achieve economies of scale and compatibility of information processes and flows at all levels. There are a number of software packages for all these levels of usage, which should be carefully evaluated by the teachers and the school administration to assess their completeness, their adaptability to the school's reality and the level of support offered by the software vendors.

Role of Digital ICTs

Digital ICTs are quickly becoming more accessible, but it is important to note that earlier technologies continue to play a critical role in education worldwide. Access to films, videotapes, telephones, television or radio is still far more commonplace than access to a computer or to the Internet and the World Wide Web. For example, the Telesecundaria Project in Mexico, which began in 1965 as a closed-circuit television pilot project, today delivers classes designed for lower secondary school level to over 12,000 rural communities, enrolling more than 800,000 students.

The new digital ICTs are not single technologies, but combinations of hardware, software, media, and delivery systems. As will be seen, ICTs in education today encompass a wide range of rapidly evolving technologies, including hardware, software and applications.

New ICTs differ in several important dimensions from older technologies: they can integrate multiple media into single educational applications; they are interactive and include the capacity to control, manipulate, and contribute to the information environment; they are flexible, offering freedom from rigid scheduling and from barriers of time and location; through connectivity, they provide access to every other person on the planet who has an Internet account, to hundreds of thousands of information archives, and to millions of Web pages. These four dimensions—integration of multiple media, interactivity, flexibility of use, and connectivity—distinguish digital ICTs from previous technologies. Because of these differences, educators are finding powerful new ways to integrate digital ICTs into the curricula.

Although there is apparently no comprehensive data on ICTs in schools worldwide, it is clear from many national examples that schools are increasingly being equipped with them. It is also apparent that ICT equipment and Internet connectivity is still much more widespread in North American schools than elsewhere. For example, in the United States, the ratio of students per computer dropped from 63:1 in 1985 to 6:1 in 1997 while the number of schools with Internet access has grown from 35% in 1994 to 72% in 1997.

In Europe, more than 80% of schools in Slovenia have access to the Internet—93% of secondary schools and 80% of primary schools—which is similar to the percentages of developed countries. The Government of the United Kingdom plans to connect all schools, colleges, universities, libraries, and as many community centres as possible to the Internet by 2002. The German Government will connect 10,000 schools to the Internet by mid-1999. In Italy, plans were announced in 1998 for the installation of computer and multimedia facilities in 15,000 Italian schools to be completed by the year 2000.

In Asia, similar developments are taking place. In Japan, as of 1997, over 94% of public schools were computer-equipped and 10% were connected to the Internet. The Government plans to achieve a pupilto-computer ratio of 2:1 in middle schools and 1:1 in high schools by 1999. All of the public schools in Japan will be connected to the Internet by 2003.

In the People's Republic of China, the central government will increase funding for basic, vocational and higher education projects over the next two years. These plans include strategies to make increasing use of Internet-based educational programmes. In New Zealand, 83% of primary schools and 94% of secondary schools have Internet access.

In Latin America, the Chilean government established the Enlaces (Links) project to connect schools and related institutions to Chile's national computer network. By 1996, over 180 primary schools and 62 secondary schools had been connected and, by the year 2000, the Chilean government plans to connect 50% of the 8,250 primary schools and 100% of the 1,700 secondary schools.

In Africa, the Creating Learning Networks for African Teachers Initiative aims to contribute to educational change by encouraging educational institutions to become information and learning resource centres for their communities. It also hopes to contribute to attitudinal change among teachers with a view to stimulating ongoing professional development by creating electronic learning networks among teacher training institutions and their partners in education at local, national and international levels.

These networks will allow for exchange of information, experiences and expertise, for collaborative action and for new patterns of communication. Pilot projects were initiated in Zimbabwe by connecting five teacher training centres (TTC) and their partner institutions to the Internet. Currently the project is carried out in close collaboration with the World Bank's WorldLinks for Development programme. A project in Senegal is structured in a similar way, while in Kenya and Uganda the Initiative is being introduced as part of a collaborative learning project in the area of science/mathematics teaching, linking teachers, students and researchers in Zimbabwe, Kenya and Uganda.

In the Middle East, as part of a programme sponsored by the World Bank to improve basic education, the Turkish Government will be installing computer laboratories in over 15,000 schools and training over 200,000 teachers in computer literacy and computer-aided instruction techniques. Informal and non-formal education institutions are also increasingly being equipped with ICTs and connected to the Internet. At present, about 20% of libraries in the United Kingdom are connected to the Internet.

The government's National Grid for Learning initiative will connect all libraries and museums in the United Kingdom to the Internet. In the United States, a 1998 survey found that 73% of the nation's public libraries offered basic Internet access to the public. Many public and privately-funded museums are offering ICT-based learning opportunities. For example, in a joint project with the Fraunhofer Institute for Software and Systems Engineering, the German Historical Museum in Berlin and the Haus der Geschichte of the Federal Republic of Germany in Bonn are developing a virtual exhibition of German history for the Internet.

Community schools are also making more use of ICTs. The Lighthouse Project in Thailand is offering non-formal educational programmes at five locations in Thailand. In part, efforts to connect educational organisations to the Internet are being driven by societal pressure. This does not eliminate, however, the need to check whether there will be positive consequences for such a move. One aspect of this question is how effective the ICTs are in education. To answer this question three aspects must be considered. The first deals with the comparison between traditional teaching techniques and those which make use of ICTs; here the term ICT-mediated instruction will be used. The second covers teaching activities which would not be possible without modern ICTs, hence the expression ICT-enabled instruction. The third concerns all the techniques, whether ICT-mediated or enabled, and raises the question as to whether they are worth their costs.

The first question to be considered about the effectiveness of ICT in education is what impact, if any, ICT-mediated instruction has on student performance. ICT-mediated instruction refers to instruction delivered through a technological channel such as television, radio, or a computer network. Evidence has consistently shown that ICT mediated instruction using conventional teaching methods is as effective as traditional face-to-face instruction and, in the case of computer-based instruction, may in certain instances improve student learning and attitudes to learning.

However, the picture is less clear—but promising—for more sophisticated uses of ICTs in the classroom, especially for the host of applications and methods that support 'constructivist' learning, in which students are encouraged to work in rich environments of information and experience to build their own understanding of them. Research into the effectiveness of ICT-mediated instruction is continuing worldwide, and should provide a clearer picture of the effectiveness of ICTs in supporting constructivist teaching.

A second way to assess the merit of ITC-use in education is to consider what, if anything, they enable students and teachers to do that they would not otherwise be able to do. To explore this question, five aspects of the educational use of ICTs will be considered: supporting new teaching methods, accessing remote resources, enabling collaboration, extending educational programmes and information literacy.

New Teaching Methods

Modern constructivist educational theory emphasises critical thinking, problem solving, 'authentic' learning experiences, social negotiation of knowledge, and collaboration. The teaching methods concerned change the role of the teacher from a disseminator of information to a learning facilitator, helping students as they actively engage with information and materials to construct their own understanding. ICTs have the potential to be used in support of these new educational methods, enabling students to learn by doing.

ICTs can make it possible for teachers to provide students with self-paced, self-directed problem-based or constructivist learning experiences, as well as to test student learning in new, interactive, and attractive ways that may better assess the depth of their understanding of content and processes. One example may help illustrate how ICTs can support constructivist teaching methods. Computer Supported Intentional Learning Environments (CSILE), developed at the Ontario Institute for Studies in Education, is a network system that provides support for collaborative learning and inquiry within a school.

CSILE promotes student interaction through referencing, connecting ideas, sharing authorship, and 'building on' the work of others to advance knowledge. The central feature of CSILE is a 'communal' database into which students can enter text and graphics, and can read, add to, and comment on the work of others.

Connectivity is one of the main differences between older and newer ICTs. The first aspect of connectivity concerns access to material resources. Digital library initiatives that will provide collections that are electronically accessible on the Internet, including printed works, photographs, films and videotapes, paintings, 3D models, graphics, animations, software, reference materials, audio files, and so forth are being undertaken in countries around the world.

Thousands of websites that contain collections of high quality curriculum guides, lesson plans, and instructional activities now exist. For example, the United Nations CyberSchoolBus website contains teaching units on urbanisation, health, the environment, and women and politics, as well as interactive games, maps, databases, and quizzes. In addition to efforts to digitise existing physical resources, many new information resources (e.g. websites, digital images, electronic journals and newsletters) are being created which can only be accessed electronically. As digital representations of physical resources are created, and as more information resources are distributed in digital format only, it will be critical that students and teachers have ICT access.

Since not all resources are inanimate, a second important aspect of connectivity deals with human resources. ICT enables educational collaboration between individuals and groups of people. E-mail, computer-mediated conferencing, and desktop videoconferencing are all being used to support collaboration among individuals and groups. Collaboration is also taking place by means of realtime chat systems; whiteboards; newsgroups; computer-mediated conferencing (CMC); and specialised software like CaMILE: Collaborative and Multimedia Interactive Learning Environment and The Knowledge Integration Environment.

Other applications include MUDs (Multi-User Domains) MOOs (Multi-user Object Oriented domains), and MUSHs (Multi-User Shared Hallucinations). Such applications are Internet accessible, text-mediated virtual environments in which participants can both interact with others and help construct the common virtual space. ICTs make it possible for people in widely dispersed locations to participate in 'virtual learning communities.' Virtual learning communities are learning groups based on shared purpose, rather than on distinctions of location or age.

Through the ICTs, learners can be drawn together from almost anywhere in the world, and can construct their own formal or informal learning groups. Such communities may cross barriers of time, geography, age, ability, culture and social status. Virtual education allows students to study at their own time, place and pace. In essence, a virtual education means having educational transactions accessible from the home, the workplace or anywhere that the student chooses to be. Virtual Design Studios, begun in 1993, are a form of collaboration among teams of architecture students in universities worldwide.

Teachers and students, on different continents and in different time zones, work on common design projects using computer-aided design systems, e-mail, a central database, and videoconferencing. Participants use the World Wide Web to display their designs and a virtual international jury of architects and teachers judges the relative merit of the work. Virtual Design Studio techniques are also being utilised by other disciplines, such as engineering.

The SIMULAB Project, supported by the European Union, involves web-based communication among language students across national boundaries. Using specialised software, teachers can create Internet-based simulations for role-playing activities in language learning. The simulations, incorporating e-mail, chat, and online creation and editing of documents, are thought to motivate oral and written communication among the participating groups, while students are guided through scenarios relevant to the country of their chosen language.

ICTs make it possible to extend the reach of educational programmes in two important ways. First, educational programmes can be delivered anywhere in the world. Second, ICTs can help individuals learn throughout their lifetime. Distance education programmes, also known as 'distributed' education programmes, are those in which the teacher and students are physically separated, and teaching and learning takes place by means of single technologies or combinations of ICTs. In the past, such programmes made use of print, radio, and television.

Today, new ICTs are leading to changes in these traditional 'open' or distance education programmes. For example, the International Francophone Consortium of Distance and Open Learning Institutions (CIFFAD), a consortium of open and distance learning institutions spread over 49 countries, of which 80% are in developing nations, has recently entered into a phase of re-engineering to make use of new ICTs. The group aims to provide at least one hundred access points to the Internet per year in member establishments with the major part of the consortium having access to the network by the end of 1998.

In the Pacific region, the University of the South Pacific has been using Intelsat for several years. The Western

Governors University is an example of a 'virtual university', or university with no physical campus. WGU, initiated in 1996 by 18 governors in the western United States, offers more than 300 college-level distance learning courses from 30 affiliated universities and education providers. WGU has forged international alliances with the China Internet Education Center, Tokai University in Japan, the University of British Columbia in Canada, the Open University in the United Kingdom and the Virtual University of the Monterrey Institute of Technology in Mexico. The principal aim is to collaborate on the development and delivery of distance learning programmes.

In Germany, the four Baden universities, namely, Freiburg, Karlsruhe, Mannheim and Heidelberg, recently announced the establishment of that country's first virtual university. The objective is to establish individual distance learning via e-mail Integrated Services Digital Networks (ISDN) or digital television. In Africa, the World Bank is funding the development of the African Virtual University (AVU). AVU completed a pilot phase in 1996-98 and is now moving into an operational phase when it will begin delivering full-fledged undergraduate degree programmes in science and engineering in January 1999.

The AVU's programmes will be delivered by a combination of ICTs including interactive television and the Internet. The programme is developing a digital library of scientific engineering as a resource for students and teachers. The Hanoi Summit entrusted the creation of a francophone virtual university to the Agence Universitaire de la Francophonie for a budget of 4 million French francs. As a beginning, six digitised campuses have been opened in Bulgaria, Cameroon, Haiti, Madagascar, Senegal and Viet Nam.

Virtual educational programmes are not limited to postsecondary education. The United States Department of Education has funded the Virtual High School (VHS) project. During the 1997/98 school year, VHS offered 29 Internet-based, credit-bearing courses to about 500 students in 27 schools located in 10 states. This approach is thought to be particularly useful as many of the participating schools either have no qualified teacher or insufficient enrollment to justify individually offering some of the courses which are available through this collaborative scheme.

In addition to educational institutions using ICTs to enhance or create distance learning programmes, commercial companies are offering ICT-based distance education programmes. Although alternate and distance education providers currently make up less than 2% of the postsecondary education market, almost $2 billion dollars has been raised on Wall Street since 1996 to finance such new ventures. Establishing lifelong learning habits among citizens and providing lifelong learning opportunities has become a major goal of governments and nongovernmental organisations worldwide.

For example, UNESCO's Learning Without Frontiers (LWF) initiative, 'is geared towards stimulating innovation and exploring alternative pathways/partners/technologies for the provision of lifelong and lifewide learning opportunities, particularly, to those who are currently unreached by or excluded from conventional modes of educational delivery'. In addition to this initiative, UNESCO has recently set up an Institute for Information Technologies in Education (IITE), located in Moscow and designed to act as an international clearing-house for the collection and dissemination of best practices and models in the field of application of information and communication technologies in education.

It will also offer assistance in the pre- and in-service training of the teachers in the use of information technology, particularly in the developing countries, countries in transition and countries of the Commonwealth of Independent States. The European Lifelong Learning Initiative makes use of ICTs, 'to initiate the dissemination of information, the coordination of projects and studies, the mobilisation of actions, people and organisations to bring Europe into the Lifelong Learning Age. It covers all sectors and all countries'.

In the light of changing perceptions about what constitutes appropriate skills for the modern era, some organisations are promulgating educational standards that attempt to define what all students should know about ICTs. For example, the National Educational Technology Standards (NETS) project in the United States has released an initial set of national educational technology standards for precollege students. However, although it may be assumed that students will have to acquire new skills in order to compete and contribute in an increasingly ICT dominated global economy, it is not clear what skills will be necessary: 'Unlike the more stable content and goals we have for other areas of school study, technology continues to change and evolve; with these changes come ever-new goals for how technology should serve learning, and what students should know about technology'.

There does seem to be a growing consensus that all students must achieve 'information literacy': 'It is the task of general education to provide every girl and boy with the versatile basic skills in acquiring, managing and communicating information which are necessary in the information society and essential for successful further study'. Focusing on concepts such as 'information literacy', rather than on specific technologies or applications, may be essential in planning and developing new curricula.

Cost-effectiveness

The third issue when assessing the effectiveness of ICT in education is the question of cost-effectiveness. Information is of critical importance, especially to developing countries with fewer resources to invest. However, assessing the cost-effectiveness of ICTs in education is difficult, if not impossible, for at least four reasons: lack of meaningful data, variability in the use of ICTs, difficulty of generalising from specific programmes, and difficulty of assessing the value of qualitative educational differences. In addition, traditional cost-analyses cannot take into account the societal and economic consequences of not investing in ICTs for education.

Nonetheless, even in the face of such obstacles, attempts to establish the relative costs of ICTs in education have been reported. In general, these studies find that the use of new ICTs is more expensive than instruction delivered by older technologies like print and radio, but less expensive than instruction delivered by television. In a World Bank report on education and ICTs in Latin America and the Caribbean, the costs of using a computer with an Internet connection in a school was much less expensive per pupil than broadcast television, but substantially more expensive than radio. M. Potashnik and D. Adkins, in spite of severe lack of data, were able to compare the per pupil costs of setting up a computer laboratory in a school for computer-assisted instruction in Belize ($78), Jamaica ($89), and Chile ($104). A similar analysis of the costs of equipping a classroom, not a laboratory, with computers in the United States for computer-assisted instruction yielded a figure of $453.

L. Osin, in a paper on ICTs in developing countries, assessed the annual per-student cost of providing computers for instruction in developing countries at $84. This finding is in close agreement with the study by Potashnik and Adkins mentioned above. On the same basis, if 30 computers were used 300 days per year, 10 hours per day, as a resource to raise the skills and education levels of all members of the community, not just students, Osin estimates the cost would decrease to $0.34 per hour of interaction. He concludes, 'There is no alternative system known that may provide the benefits possible by integrating computers in the education system, while at the same time serving the whole community'.

Another factor that must be considered when calculating the cost-effectiveness of ICT use is the question of alternatives. The costs of building sufficient campuses to handle the rising demand for education may be prohibitive. Virtual educational institutions do not require the same campus infrastructure and related costs incurred by campusbased institutions. In Taipei (Taiwan, China), the distance educationbased National Open University, with its budget of NT$800 million, accommodates approximately 30,000 adult students each year.

By comparison, the National Taiwan University, one of the larger universities in Taipei, has an annual budget of $NT3,500 million for its 21,000 students. Though gross numbers of this sort beg some level of refinement, the differential costs remain substantial and manifest.

Lastly, when discussing cost-effectiveness, the societal costs to developing countries of not preparing their citizens to participate in an information-based global society must be considered. The World Development Report 1998/99 warns that the global explosion of knowledge may either lift hundreds of millions of the world's poor out of poverty or it may create a widening knowledge gap, in which poor countries lag further and further behind.

As Potashnik and Adkins have pointed out, 'even in countries which do not believe in the cost-effectiveness of information technology as a tool for mass education, it is important that they begin acquiring experience using this technology for educational purposes. Otherwise, educators in developing countries will be marginalised in the international dialogue on education'.

ICT-ENABLED LEARNING ENVIRONMENTS

Infrastructure

In order to make use of digital ICTs, schools must be equipped with computers. In order to access the Internet from a computer, schools, homes, libraries, and other educational venues must be equipped with an Internet connection, either by means of the telephone or cable network and a modem or a direct connection. Many creative means of providing computers and building the necessary Internet infrastructure are being explored in countries throughout the world.

Education/business Collaboration

Collaboration, including cost sharing, between education and industry to build ICT infrastructure is becoming commonplace. For example, the Bristol Education Online Network (BEON) project and the follow-on Merseyside Education Online Network (MEON) are co-operative efforts of the commercial companies British Telecom (BT) and International Computers Limited (ICL), local schools and the University of Exeter School of Education.

ICL is supplying multimedia computers and BT is providing access to remote services and to the Internet to a number of schools in the area. Another promising approach to equipping schools with computers inexpensively is to transfer the technology from government organisations and businesses to schools. For example, the Computers for Schools programme in Canada, is soliciting donations of 'obsolete' or redundant computers from business, industry, and individuals, and refurbishing them before donating them to schools.

Netdays Initiatives

Netday initiatives, which began in 1995, are characterised as 'high-tech barn-raising,' in other words, efforts by community volunteers to wire classrooms, libraries, and computer laboratories so that they may connect to the Internet. *Organisers of such efforts typically help schools to* develop a technical plan that includes instructional goals, network and wiring architecture, network management and technical support, training, and an operating budget.

On a specific day, volunteers from the local community do the physical work necessary to set up the network, greatly reducing the costs of providing Internet access within the schools. Netdays now take place in many countries including Australia, New Zealand, European countries, Israel, Japan, and South Africa. In Latin American and the Caribbean, UNESCO is sponsoring a netday initiative.

Community Networking Initiatives

Many community networking initiatives have educational components and are worthy of mention. In an interesting example of how community networking can benefit educational institutions, the International Telecomputing Consortium is working with schools and universities in China to create school-based community networks. In these projects, schools establish computer centres with Internet access for use by students and teachers in class. After hours, the centre remains open and training by teachers and students is made available to parents and other members of the community who may not have Internet access. The school thus provides Internet access for the community with some revenue returning to the school.

Importance of Content

Beyond equipment and software, appropriate content is necessary to make use of ICTs for educational purposes. Although some online content is specifically designed for educational purposes, most is not. One approach to facilitating access to appropriate educational content is the creation of a 'Schoolnet'. Schoolnets, also known as 'national education grids', are local, national or regional projects that may include efforts to wire schools physically to information services, but the fundamental aim is to provide access to appropriate educational content.

For example, the United Kingdom's National Grid for Learning (NGfL) 'is both an architecture (or structure) of educationally valuable content on the Internet, and a programme for developing the means to access that content in schools, libraries, colleges, universities, workplaces, homes and elsewhere'. Schoolnets now exist in France, Ireland, Japan, South Africa, Thailand, and other countries. One of the advantages of new ICTs is that they empower users not only to consume information, but also to produce it. With a computer, printer, and desktop publishing software, any local educational group can produce high quality printed materials.

With an Internet connection and a website, any educational organisation can 'publish' content derived from local knowledge and experience. For example, the Summer Institute of Linguistics (SIL) has helped set-up Literacy and Awareness Publication (LAMP) centres in each of the twenty provinces of Papua New Guinea to promote literacy in approximately 850 local languages. At these centres, literacy texts are produced that can be shared between the centres; they cover a wide variety of subjects including healthcare, hygiene and preservation of the environment.

Although many tools exist to help teachers and students locate information, at present finding specific educational materials on the World Wide Web can be likened to a scavenger hunt, often resulting in wasted time and unexpected results. A teacher or student may find it difficult to locate specific information or materials that might be useful within the curriculum at a particular grade level. The results of indiscriminate searches also raise the issue of the validity and reliability of the information let alone legality and harmfulness.

Because of varying technical standards, materials created with one ICTbased learning system may not be usable in a different technical environment once they have been found. Several efforts to bring order to the chaos of the Internet and World Wide Web are underway. To this end, the European Commission has initiated a Memorandum of Understanding: Multimedia Access to Education and Training in Europe. By December 1998, over 160 educational organisations, government agencies, and commercial companies had signed the MoU.

Projects like the Dublin Core Metadata Initiative and the Instructional Management Systems (IMS) project which create technical standards, may 'help transform the end-user experience of the Web from the unstructured tangle it is today into something more like a digital library or virtual learning centre'. If international agreement can be reached on an acceptable set of technical standards, teachers and students may be able to search for educational materials with common descriptors and be assured that the materials, once found, will be compatible with local ICT applications.

Teacher Training

As noted in a Finnish government report, 'how computers are used in education depends on the pedagogical competence and technical skills of the teaching staff who must know how to exploit these modern technologies in pedagogically meaningful ways'. In some countries, for example the United Kingdom, training in ICT use is a requirement for a teaching certificate. As educational applications of ICT continue to evolve, apart from preparatory training, refresher courses for experienced teachers will also be necessary. Furthermore, it may not be sufficient simply to provide training for teachers.

For instance, Murphy and Gunter advocate that ICT training be extended to educational administrators. ICT training for teachers must deal with at least two aspects. First, teachers need technical training to learn how to use and maintain ICT equipment and software. Such technical training is being offered to teachers in a wide variety of ways. Pre-service university-based courses, in-service workshops, commercial training programmes, and other opportunities abound, many of which make use of ICTs to deliver the training. Second, since 'integration of technologies into curricula requires changes of huge magnitude', training in how to integrate ICT use into the curriculum is necessary.

Such training should include effective ICT teaching methods and the use of discipline-specific applications. In one possible framework for organising ICT training for teachers, McDougall and Squires identify five areas: skills with particular applications; integration into existing curricula; ICT-related changes in curricula; changes in teachers' roles; and underpinning theories of education. The authors note that most ICT teacher training mistakenly focuses entirely on the first issue. Many innovative approaches are being developed to provide support for university staff. For example, several universities have established 'expert partners' programmes.

As reported by Guernsey, 'people who fill the jobs have one thing in common: a hybrid expertise that blends academic computing with college teaching'. Staff who are both qualified academics within a discipline and who have expertise using ICTs for instruction are hired 'to provide faculty on-site, intradepartmental consulting and support in information and instructional technology for academic purposes to foster their awareness and use of technological resources, both within and without the University'. In another innovative but more costly approach, students are being enlisted to provide ICT support and training for teachers. At Wake Forest University (North Carolina) in the United States, firstyear students are hired and trained to work as Student Technology AdvisoRS (STARS).

STARS are assigned to faculty members to help implement ICT-based projects. Training methodologies vary, but 'training of trainers' models are common and in most instances may be more cost-effective than on-site, small group or individual ICT training. In such programmes, 'teacher-leaders' are selected using a variety of criteria such as prior experience with ICTs in education, staff development expertise, and the commitment to the programme by school and district administration. These individuals receive intensive training courses to master technical details and approaches to integrating ICTs into the curricula.

Once trained, they return to their educational institutions and provide ICT training and support for their peers. Such programmes may also include ongoing, longterm support for the trainers, including site visits, computer-based conferences, and e-mail advice. In large geographical areas, the responsibility for such training and continuing support may be delegated to regional ICT consortia co-ordinated by a central administrative body.

The provision of on-site, technical support as needed is critical to the success of an ICT-based educational programme. Although standard service agreements, purchased separately or included in the purchase of ICT equipment and software, typically cover regular maintenance and repair costs, and may even include e-mail or telephone support, such arrangements may fall short of what is necessary in educational settings. Without adequate technical support, schools have experienced 'large workloads for existing staff, maintenance backlogs, and reduced computer use because computers were out of service'. In universities, such support may take the form of technical staff assigned to a 'computer centre', 'media centre', or 'distance learning centre'. In schools, knowledgeable peers, students, volunteers and specialised computer teachers are generally providing such support; less frequently, trained technical staff, located either within the school or district office, are employed.

The use of ICTs in education is a difficult, expensive and complex undertaking and a host of issues, including infrastructure, curricula changes, teacher training, technical support, and so on must be considered. Such an undertaking, especially on a national level, requires careful planning. Many governments stand at the threshold of the twenty-first century without clearly-defined plans and strategies about the use of educational technology—but they are making major new investments anyway. The report identifies generic issues for planners to consider when developing national ICT education strategies. These are broadly grouped into three categories: educational policy and goals setting, teaching and learning, and institutional development and capacity building.

The report also itemises several successful strategies, implemented in varying degrees, including developing a national or regional plan for country-wide deployment of technologies; implementing experimental projects to gain experience for country-wide deployment; undertaking small-scale demonstration projects; using technology to address educational equity issues; using broadcast technologies, including computer networks, to reach learners in remote areas; investing in preparing students and teachers for technology-based jobs; and creating schools using ICT as their core educational delivery system. Claeys, Lowych, and Van der Perre, in an article based on interviews with a sample of 65 experts from across Europe about introducing ICTs into education, summarise the respondents' view of the role of government as that of developing a clear vision on reforming the educational system through ICTs, enacting adequate funding measures, and establishing partnerships with education and industry for the development of educational software.

Osin, summarising the experiences of projects in developed countries, warns against beginning a project by purchasing computers. He advocates an eight-step planning process beginning with gathering together the necessary expertise in an Advisory Committee that will define and implement a plan which starts by the careful implementation of pilot projects. Osin also recommends training a cadre of instructors for teacher training, introducing computers into teacher-training colleges, and conducting both formative and summary evaluations of the pilot projects before attempting large-scale ICT implementation.

Apart from planning, national governments have a role to play in helping to remove political and economic roadblocks that prevent the sharing of educational resources among countries. McIsacc and Blocher, in a discussion of distance education, advocate: 'Courses offered globally should encourage broad international participation and have sliding scale tuition policies. Sharing in developing educational materials and courses saves the duplication of time and effort and conserves valuable national resources'. Potashnik and Capper, in their article, note:

Employers and universities are now drawing both staff members and students from all corners of the globe. Consequently, they face new challenges in evaluating course work done at, and degrees earned from, unknown institutions in other countries. While accreditation has typically been controlled by individual countries, the globalisation of distance education has created a whole new challenge in accreditation and certification of learning. These authors continue, citing the Global Alliance for Transnational Education (GATE), an international alliance of higher education, government and business, as one effort 'to carry out the formidable task of creating a global certification and review process for education delivered across borders'.

Government intervention may also help assure affordable ICT access for education. For example, telecommunications rates may be regulated to assure economical ICT access to educational institutions. In late 1996, the United States Congress enacted the Telecommunications Act of 1996. The universal service section of the law, Section 254, will help schools and libraries obtain access to telecommunications services and technologies at discounted rates. Tax incentives, such as the 21st Century Classrooms Act for Private Technology Investment, enacted by the United States Congress in 1997, are one way of encouraging corporate ICT-equipment donations to educational institutions.

The Act allows companies to deduct the full price of a computer which is donated to a school within two years of purchase from their taxes. ICTs are evolving rapidly and, once established, national educational policies on ICT 'have to be regularly updated if they are to respond adequately to the challenge of effectively exploiting these constant changes to the technologies and their applications'.

2

ICT-Use in Education

Communication and information are at the very heart of the educational process. Information and communication technologies (ICTs) has played an educational role in formal and non-formal settings, in programmes provided by governmental agencies, public and private educational institutions, for-profit corporations and non-profit groups, and secular and religious communities. Much has been written about the use of film, radio, telephones, and television in education. Because access to digital tools, applications, and networks continues to grow worldwide and media are increasingly available in digital form, ICT-use in education can be expected to increase dramatically.

The ability to digitise analog signals and transmit them over telecommunications networks is resulting in the restructuring of the radio, telephone, television, publishing, entertainment, and computer industries into new multimedia industries that create digital products combining voice, video, text, graphics, images, and animations, and deliver these signals electronically.

Our emphasis also mirrors the increasing access to digital tools and resources worldwide. Although estimating the number of people with Internet access is difficult at best, one current estimate places the total number at around 150 million in late 1998, an increase of over 60% since early 1997. Internet access is at present strongly concentrated in a small number of countries, providing services to a fraction of the world's population: over 90% of Internet hosts are located in the world's richest 29 counties. However, this may be expected to change over time as telecommunications costs continue to drop precipitously and governments deregulate access.

For example, the number of Internet users in India is expected to climb from half a million in 1998 to 1.5 million by the year 2000. In Africa, it is estimated that there currently are between 800,000 and 1 million Internet users. The current ratio of Internet users to people in Africa is estimated to be one for every 5,000 compared to a world average of about one Internet user to every 40 people. But here, too, the situation is rapidly changing. In 1996, only 16 countries in Africa had Internet access. Now, 53 (three-fourths) of the capital cities are online and the rest will soon follow.

A number of international infrastructure building initiatives are underway on the continent including the United Nations Secretary General's programme Harnessing Information Technology for Development that will substantially improve the Internet infrastructure by the year 2000. The Russian Non-Profit Center for Internet Technologies estimates that there are now about 1 million Russians online and that this number is doubling every year. And, in the next two years, the number of Internet users in Latin America is expected to grow from 8.5 million to about 34 million. The number of Latin American websites, most of which are operated by businesses, could triple in the next year to over 500,000.

In Asia, estimates place the total number of Chinese online in Hong Kong, Taiwan, and Singapore at 2.6 million. The number of users in China almost doubled (620,000 - 1.175 million) from late 1997 to mid-June, 1998. Some estimates predict there will be 20 million Internet users in China by the year 2000. As these few examples help illustrate, although ICT access is still chiefly available to citizens of developed countries; such access is fast becoming possible in developing countries worldwide.

Role of ICTs in Formal Education

Although no comprehensive data on ICT in schools worldwide apparently exists, it is clear from many national examples that schools are also increasingly being equipped with ICT. It is also apparent that ICT equipment and Internet connectivity is still much more abundant in North American schools than elsewhere. In the United States, the ratio of students per computer dropped from 63:1 to 6:1 from 1985 to 1997 while the number of schools with internet access has grown from 35% in 1994 to 72% in 1997.

In Africa, the Creating Learning Networks for African Teachers project, part of the UN's Harnessing Information Technology for Development initiative mentioned above, will equip a maximum of four teacher training colleges (TTCs) in each of 20 African countries with a computer and full access to the Internet. The project will also fund teacher training curriculum development and the creation of 20 national educational WWW sites.

In Europe, more than 80% of schools in Solvenia have access to the Internet—93% of secondary schools and 80% of primary schools—which is similar to the percentages of developed countries. Nearly two-thirds of secondary schools have a website. In the United Kingdom, the pupil to computer ratio is 16:1 in primary schools and 9:1 in secondary schools, while 43% of schools in the United Kingdom are connected to the Internet. The British Government plans to connect all schools, colleges, universities, libraries, and as many community centres as possible to the Internet by 2002.

In Germany, the Schulen ans Netz initiative begun in 1996, will connect 10,000 schools to the Internet by mid-1999. As of late 1997, of approximately 6,500 were connected and 1,700 had their own website. And in Italy, a national programme in 1995 resulted in 120 schools being supplied with multimedia equipment. Last year, plans were announced for the installation of computer and multimedia facilities in 15,000 Italian schools to be carried out by the year 2000. At the end of the programme, approximately 25% of all Italian state schools will have access to on-line facilities and the Internet and will be equipped with advanced hardware and multimedia educational software.

In Asia, similar developments are taking place. In Japan, as of 1997, over 94% of pubic schools were computer-equipped and 10% were connected to the Internet. The Government plans to provide a pupil to computer ratio of 2:1 in middle schools and 1:1 in high schools by 1999. All of the public schools in Japan will be connected to the Internet by 2003. In the People's Republic of China, the central government will increase funding for basic, vocational and higher education projects over the next two years. These plans include strategies to make increasing use of Internet-based educational programmes.

In South America, in 1993, the Chilean government established the Enlaces (Links) project to connect schools and related institutions to Chile's national computer network. By 1996, over180 primary schools and 62 secondary schools had been connected and, by the year 2000, the Chilean government plans to have 50% of the 8,250 primary schools and 100% of the 1,700 secondary schools connected. The Enlaces initiative also includes equipping schools with computers and a combination of locally produced educational software and commercial products that are available in Spanish language versions.

In New Zealand these few examples serve to illustrate that efforts to provide ICT and Internet access to teachers and students in developed and developing countries around the world can be expected to continue and accelerate until most, if not all, schools are equipped and connected in the next century.

Role of ICTs in Informal and Non-Formal Education

Informal and non-formal education refers to educational activities and programmes that are offered outside of formal educational institutions, including those offered by libraries, museums, community schools and centres, zoos, planetariums, commercial companies, and many other organisations. Informal and non-formal education institutions, too, are increasingly being equipped with ICT and connected to the Internet. At present, about 20% of libraries in the United Kingdom are connected to the Internet. The British government's National Grid for Learning initiative will connect all British libraries and museums to the Internet.

In the United States, a 1998 survey sponsored by the American Library Association found 73% of the nation's public libraries offered basic Internet access to the public. Many public and privately funded museums are offering

ICT-based learning opportunities. For example, the Computer Museum's website offers activities designed to help individuals learn about computers. The British Natural History Museum, as part of a European Union funded project to enable multimedia applications such as virtual museums and galleries to be accessed from remote locations, has constructed a virtual model of the Endeavour, Captain Cook's ship.

The ship, as well as virtual reality objects of seabirds and other animals encountered by Cooke on his voyages, are available on the Web. And, in a joint project with the Fraunhofer Institute for Software and Systems Engineering, the German Historical Museum in Berlin and the Haus der Geschichte of the Federal Republic of Germany in Bonn are developing a virtual exhibition of German history for the Internet. Community school efforts, too, are increasingly making use of ICTs. The Lighthouse Project in Thailand is offering nonformal educational programmes at five locations in Thailand as well as an online "community magazine," Sakura Press.

The community school-based project "initiates a challenge against the existing educational system ... The new environments and new technologies will be the main mechanism to help learners generate their own ideas, expand them, and share them with others".

Differences between Old and New Technologies

New ICTs differ in several important dimensions from older technologies, including the integration of multiple media, interactivity, flexibility of use, and connectivity. Understanding these differences will provide a clearer picture of why the use of ICT in education can be expected to continue to grow.

Integration of Multiple Media

Because of advances in digital technologies, it is now possible to integrate multiple media into single educational applications. Multimedia applications on CD-ROMs and websites may incorporate text, pictures, audio, graphics, animations, simulations, full-motion video, and links to other software or websites greatly enriching the learning experience. For example, Astronomy Village: Investigating the Universe is a CDROM-based multimedia programme developed at the NASA Classroom of the Future that contains ten complete four-week-long investigations for secondary students.

Multimedia tools available on the CD-ROM include an image-processing programme, an image browser, a telecommunications programme for accessing the World Wide Web, a star life cycle simulator, an orbital simulator, and a 3-D star simulator. Multimedia resources include 85 minutes of digitised video clips; more than 300 images from the Hubble Space Telescope and other instruments; 12 illustrated audio lectures by astronomers discussing their work; over 100 computer animations and graphics; and 180 full text documents such as book chapters, NASA publications, and articles from astronomy journals and magazines.

Interactivity

Earlier technologies used for instruction were passive in nature. That is, the delivery of instruction required no action on the part of students beyond listening, watching, and perhaps taking notes. Such ICTs were one-way channels of instructional delivery. New ICTs give the student and teacher the ability to control, manipulation, and contribute to the information environment. On the lowest and least valuable level, this may simply mean the student controls the pace and order of a presentation. But much more is possible. Using ICT students may not only make choices about the pace and order of a presentation, but may choose topics; take notes; answer questions; explore virtual landscapes; enter, draw or chart data; run simulated experiments; create and manipulate images; make their own multimedia presentations, communicate with others, and more.

Flexibility of Use

Previously, ICT-use required students to be grouped together in a controlled environment at a specific time and location. With some technologies, for example radio and television, use was rigidly tied to schedules developed by people far removed from the day-to-day functioning of the classroom. New ICT applications have given rise to the term "anytimeanyplace," a reflection of the flexibility possible in using ICT to support teaching and learning. One outgrowth of this flexibility has been the development of "virtual" educational experiences.

A virtual experience refers to educational situations in which distance and time separate the teacher and students, who use ICT to interactively to share resources, communicate, and learn. Virtual education allows students to study at their own time, place and pace. In essence, a virtual education means having educational transactions accessible from the home, workplace, or anywhere that the student chooses to be. Virtual classrooms, schools, colleges, and universities offering classes by email, computer-mediated conferencing (CMC), videoconferencing, or websites, or combinations of these technologies, are proliferating.

Connectivity

Perhaps the most powerful feature of new ICTs is connectivity. Prior to the 1990s, computers in educational settings were seldom connected to local area networks (LANs) or the Internet. With the widespread adoption of LANs, decreasing telecommunications costs, increasing bandwidth, and the invention of the World Wide Web, educational access to the Internet is becoming commonplace. If equipped with a computer, appropriate software, and Internet access, students and teachers have access to every other person on the planet who has an Internet account, hundreds of thousands of information archives, and millions of webpages of educationally relevant content. These four dimensions—integration of multiple media, interactivity, flexibility of use, and connectivity—distinguish digital ICT from previous technologies. Because of these differences, educators are finding powerful new ways to integrate digital ICTs into the curricula.

Effects of ICTs

ICT-Mediated Instruction

The first question to be considered about the effectiveness of ICT in education is what, if any, impact ICT-mediated instruction has on student performance. ICT-mediated instruction refers to instruction delivered via a technological channel such as television, radio, or a computer and network. ICT-mediated instruction can be synchronous, with both the instructor and the student participating simultaneously. For example, instruction may be delivered via desktop videoconferencing by a teacher located at a university to employees at widely separated companies.

ICT-mediated instruction may also be delivered asynchronously, with the instructor and student participating at different times. Instruction based on teaching materials placed on a website does not requiring simultaneous participation. Or synchronicity may not matter, as when self-contained instructional materials are packaged on a CD-ROM. In this case, the instructional designer may have developed the materials months or even years before the student uses them and communication between the two is impossible.

Early studies of ICT-mediated instruction's effect on student learning have been characterised as the "no significant difference" phenomena. That is to say, whatever medium of instructional delivery—film, radio, television, telephone, or computer—was used, no significant difference on performance measures was found between students receiving ICT-mediated instruction and those receiving traditional face-to-face instruction in a classroom. Both groups perform equally well. Studies focusing on the use of computer-mediated instruction conducted in the 1980s found more positive results. In a meta-analysis of over 500 individual studies, James Kulik found:

1. Students usually learn more in classes in which they receive computer-based instruction ...
2. Students learn their lessons in less time with computer-based instruction ...
3. Students also like their classes more when they receive computer help in them ...

4. Students develop more positive attitudes toward computers when they receive help from them in school ...

5. Computers do not, however, have positive effects in every area in which they were studied. The average effect of computer-based instruction in 34 studies of attitude toward subject matter was near zero ...

Kulik's meta-analyses were conducted on studies of computer use prior to the 1990s. Such use was often limited to drill and practice and tutorial software programmes. In the 1990s, use of ICT in schools is moving toward engaging students in "authentic" learning tasks in which students use computers, software, and network access to simulate events, communicate, collaborate, analyse data and access information resources. For these applications of ICT in schools, the research data are less extensive. However, some individual studies have been conducted that demonstrate positive learning and affective outcomes.

A recent study by ETS of student achievement in mathematics and the use of ICT—the first such study to document relationships between student use of technology across the United States and higher scores on a national standardised test—concluded that "technology does matter to academic achievement, with the important caveat that whether it matters depends upon how it is used". In another recent study undertaken by the Bertelsmann Foundation of students in a German school and a school in the United States concluded "that the use of media and technology improves learning outcomes, instills key qualifications for the information age, and increases motivation". And finally, one concern often expressed about ICT is that its use will isolate students from each other and from their teachers.

In a 10-year longitudinal study undertaken by Apple Computer, "Dispelling widespread myths, the researchers found that instead of isolating students, access to technology actually encouraged them to collaborate more than in traditional classrooms. And instead of becoming boring with use, technology was even more interesting to students as they began using it for creating and communicating". It appears, therefore, that ICT, properly used, may enhance and increase communications between people. In conclusion, evidence has consistently shown ICT-mediated instruction using conventional teaching methods is as good as traditional face-to-face instruction and, in the case of computer-based instruction, may in select instances improve student learning and attitudes towards learning.

However, the picture is less clear—but promising—for more sophisticated uses of ICT in the classroom, especially for the host of applications and methods that support "constructivist" learning, in which students are encouraged to work in rich environments of information and experience to build their own understandings about them. Worldwide, research into the effectiveness of ICT-mediated instruction is continuing and should provide a clearer picture of the effectiveness of ICT in supporting constructivist pedagogy. For example, as part of the Helsinki 2000 project, Finnish investigators are conducting a five-year, multi-disciplinary investigation focused on analysing innovative pedagogical practices through intensive case studies on computer-supported collaborative learning.

ICT-Enabled Education

A second way to assess the merit of ITC-use in education is to consider what, if anything, such use enables students and teachers to do that they would not otherwise be able to do. To explore this question, we consider five aspects of the educational use of ICT—supporting new pedagogical methods, accessing remote resources, enabling collaboration, extending educational programmes, and developing skills for the workplace.

Supporting new pedagogical methods

Modern constructivist educational theory emphasises critical thinking, problem solving, "authentic" learning experiences, social negotiation of knowledge, and collaboration—pedagogical methods that change the role of the teacher from disseminator of information to learning facilitator, helping students as they actively engage with information and materials to construct their own understandings. That is, students learn how to learn, not just what to learn. ICT has the potential to be used in support of these new educational methods, as tools enabling students' learning by doing.

ICT can make it possible for teachers to engage students in self-paced, self-directed problem-based or constructivist learning experiences; and also test student learning in new, interactive, and engaging ways that may better assess deep understanding of content and processes. Two examples may help illustrate how ICT can support constructivist teaching methods. Computer Supported Intentional Learning Environments (CSILE), developed at the Ontario Institute for Studies in Education, is a network system that provides support for collaborative learning and inquiry within a school.

CSILE promotes student interaction through referencing, connecting ideas, sharing authorship, and "building-on" the work of others to advance knowledge. The central feature of CSILE is a "communal" database into which students can enter text and graphics, and can read, add to, and comment on other's work. The commercial version of CSILE, Knowledge Base, is being used in both work and educational settings in Canada, Japan, the United States, Finland, and the Netherlands. The Physics Teaching Studio, pioneered at the Rensselaer Polytechnic Institute in the United States, incorporates the systematic use of ICT in a cooperative learning environment for instruction in undergraduate physics.

Laboratory data acquisition and analysis tools are *embedded into a hypermedia text that introduces scientific* topics, links the students to related materials, and poses questions for the students to answer with the ICT tools. Studio courses emphasise a hands-on, learning by doing approach engaging students in various problem solving and active learning sessions. This approach has been applied to mathematics courses and the concept has spread to other universities including City University of Hong Kong and Curtin University of Technology in Australia.

Improved assessment tools can also be developed using ICT. Such assessments can engage students in tasks that require data manipulation, simulation or other interactive acts of knowledge construction. VizQuiz is a multimedia programme that allows students to take a chemistry quiz at a computer, but with the added advantage that colour graphics, animations, and video clips can be included in the questions. In addition to multimedia capability, such programmes can provide hints, remedial feedback, worked out solutions or explanations, and instantaneous grading. However, although ICT offers the opportunity to construct powerful learning experiences, it is pedagogically neutral.

That is, instead of being used in the ways described above, ICT can be used in support of traditional teaching methodologies like the large group lecture, student note taking, and examinations. Teachers can use a computer and projector to show slides to illustrate a lecture, students can use laptop computers to take notes during the lecture, and multiple choice quizzes about the content of the lecture can be put on a website. How these new ICT tools and resources will be used is a human decision, not inherent in the technologies themselves.

Accessing remote resources

Connectivity is one of the main differences between older and new ICTs. Historically, information resources at libraries, schools, and universities have only been available within the walls of these institutions, in a wide variety of physical media, at certain times of the day, and in limited quantities. Because of advances in ICT, it is no longer necessary for students and teachers to be at a certain location at a specific time to acquire a physical object.

The Internet represents the greatest collection of human knowledge ever assembled, and it is available to every student and teacher properly equipped with ICT. An unlimited number of digital representations of physical objects can now be made available to students at any time and from any place. Digital library initiatives are being undertaken in countries around the world that will provide collections that are electronically accessible of the Internet including printed works (e.g., textbooks, journals, illustrations, maps, charts and graphs), photographs, films and videotapes, paintings, 3D models, graphics, animations, software, reference materials, audio files, and so forth.

A joint effort between the European Union and the National Science Foundation in the United States is exploring international collaboration on research to develop such libraries. Specialised collections of digital information are also being created. For example, the entire works of William Shakespeare may be accessed, searched, and downloaded from a website at the Massachusetts Institute of Technology (MIT). Web-based language dictionaries, such as the LEO English/German Dictionary, provide a means to translate words and phrases from one language to another.

The Louvre Museum's website offers visitors a virtual tour and access to digitised images of major works from its collection. The NASA Image eXchange offers access to hundreds of thousands of images taken by U.S. spacecraft of the Earth, the planets, moons, asteroids, and other extra-terrestrial bodies. Thousands of websites now exist that contain collections of high quality curriculum guides, lesson plans, and instructional activities. For example, the United Nations CyberSchoolBus website contains teaching units on urbanisation, disease, the environment, and women and politics, as well as interactive games, maps, databases, and quizzes.

Specialised websites designed to provide information and assistance in specific subject areas are also proliferating. Lingu@NET is a website developed by the British government to provide "quality-assured resources for language teachers and learners worldwide". And finally, remote access to expensive scientific instrumentation is also possible. In the United Kingdom, the Virtual Microscope of the Open University can be used by students to view slides over the Internet. The Hands-On Universe project at the Lawrence Berkeley National Laboratory, co-funded by several U.S. government agencies, has developed and piloted an educational programme that enables high school students to request their own observations from telescopes at professional observatories.

Students download digital images to their classroom computers and use powerful image processing software to visualise and analyse their data. This ability to access remote resources and use them locally, although not without negative aspects, fundamentally changes the quantity, nature, and potential uses of information resources available for educational purposes. In addition to efforts to digitise existing physical resources, many new information resources (e.g., websites, digital images, electronic journals and newsletters) are being created which can only be accessed electronically. As digital representations of physical resources are created, and as more information resources are distributed only in digital format, it will be critical that students and teachers have ICT access.

Enabling collaboration

Not all resources are inanimate. ICT enables educational collaborations between individuals and groups of people. Such collaborations may take place locally or between people in widely separated geographical locations. They may be temporary or long-term. Students may collaborate with peers in other schools, teachers may collaborate with university professors, members of the local business community may serve as mentors to students, scientists in government agencies may work with school children, and so forth. Only educational usefulness and access to ICT limit the possibilities.

Email, computer-mediated conferencing, and desktop videoconferencing are all being used to support collaboration between individuals and groups. Collaborations are also taking place by means of real-time chat systems; whiteboards; newsgroups; computer-mediated conferencing (CMC); and specialised software like CaMILE: Collaborative and Multimedia Interactive

Learning Environment and The Knowledge Integration Environment. Other applications include MUDs (Multi-User Domains) MOOs (Multi-user domain, Object Oriented), and MUSHs (Multi-User Shared Hallucinations).

Such applications are Internet-accessible, text-mediated virtual environments in which participants can both interact with others as well as help construct the common virtual space. At the University of California, Berkeley, classes in language, literature, linguistics, law, and communications are making use of such applications. Combinations of these ICT applications are also frequently used in educational programmes.

Online Experts: Many organisations offer "ask an expert" services. For example, students may send inquiries about scientific topics to working scientists at the Canadian Centre for Marine Geology of Dalhousie University and the U.S. Argonne National Laboratory. In other examples, online experts offer advice in health, weather topics,, and construction engineering. In an extreme example of how ICT can bridge distance to enable students to access remote expertise, last spring students from four universities in the U.S. and Canada and discussed physiology experiments with astronauts orbiting the Earth aboard the space shuttle Columbia.

Online Mentors: ICT can also enable mentoring programmes to provide one-on-one guidance to individuals by well-established members of a particular community. Such virtual collaborations between individuals are an effective ways for senior members of a community to teach, inspire, and support newcomers. Mentor High School in the United States offers an electronic Quest Forum in which freshmen students may discuss course options with students in the senior class.

In a project intended to increase retention of new teachers in the profession, the U.S. National Science Teachers Association is providing first year elementary teachers with experienced teachers as mentors. And in a final example of how ICT can support mentoring, the Asian American Psychological Association (AAPA) offers an electronic discussion group on which, according to the organisation's president elect Richard Suinn, "the elder researchers are logging on in a very constructive and supportive way, providing information and support to younger researchers".

Virtual Learning Communities: ICT makes it possible to engage people in widely dispersed locations in "virtual learning communities." Virtual learning communities are learning groups based on shared purpose, not artificial distinctions of location or age. Through ICT, learners can be drawn together from almost anywhere, and they can construct their own formal or informal learning groups. Such communities may transverse barriers of time, geography, age, ability, culture, and social status. ICT that supports such efforts can be as simple as email or as sophisticated as desktop videoconferencing systems.

In an example of how email is being used to enable virtual learning communities, a course titled International E-Mail Debate is being offered by professors at universities in Turkey, the United States, Germany, and the Czech Republic to promote writing skills across cultures and enhance intercultural awareness. Students enrolled in the course debate position papers on timely and relevant topics using E-mail. Virtual Design Studios, begun in 1993, are collaborations between teams of Architecture students in universities worldwide. Teachers and students, on different continents and in different time zones, work on a common design project using computer-aided design systems, email, a central database, and video-conferencing.

Participants use the World Wide Web to display their designs and a virtual international jury of architects and teachers judges the relative merit of the work. Past student projects included re-designing housing in Shanghai and designing a Center for Cultural and Religious Studies in Japan. A similar effort took place in 1996 between students and teachers at Union College (USA), METU (Turkey), and Queen's University (Canada). Virtual Design Studio techniques are being utilised by other disciplines, such as Engineering.

The Global Learning and Observations to Benefit the Environment (Globe) programme, sponsored by the U.S. Government, links students, teachers, and the scientific research community worldwide in a virtual learning community to study the global environment. Internationally, GLOBE is being implemented through bilateral agreements between the U.S. government and governments of partner nations. As of December 1998, thousands of schools in 74 countries have registered as participants. In the GLOBE programme, scientists design protocols for specific measurements they need for Earth Science research that can be performed by K-12 students.

Teachers are trained in the GLOBE protocols and teach them to their students. Students make the measurements, enter data via the Internet to a central data archive, and the data becomes available to scientists and the general community. Scientific visualisations of the data are provided over the Internet. Students benefit by having a "hands-on" experience in science, math, and technology, using their own local environment as a learning laboratory. Students also benefit from the opportunity to communicate with their peers around the world, thus increasing not only their environmental understanding but also their understanding of other cultures and their sense of global community.

Beginning in 1995, a series of online "Quest" projects have brought together students and teachers together around the world into a virtual community to learn about specific topics framed in an interactive learning expedition. For example, during MayaQuest, a 1995-96 project, over 1 million students, teachers, and others from around the globe followed the progress of a five-rider scientific bike expedition among Mayan ruins in Mexico and Central America, learning about the ancient Mayan civilisation and learning from on-site archaeologists. The bicyclists carried laptop computers and a satellite dish to connect to the Internet.

Students voted on team decisions, explored 21 Maya sites and were virtually on hand for several major archaeological discoveries. The original MayaQuest website received over a 1.2 million hits in 90 days. It offered team updates, photographs, teachers' guides, and direct interaction with eight of the world's top archaeologists. The company has since offered educational scientific expeditions to Africa and the Galapagos Islands. Other organisations are offering online learning adventures for teachers and students. The Jason Project and the Magellan Global Adventure are two other examples of such online adventures, explorations, and expeditions.

The SIMULAB Project, supported by the European Union, involves web-based communication between language students across national boundaries. Using specialised software, teachers can create Internet-based simulations for role-playing activities in language learning.

The simulations, incorporating email, chat, and online creation and editing of documents, are thought to motivate oral and written communication amongst the participating groups, while students are guided through scenarios relevant to the country of their chosen language.

The UNICEF Voices of Youth website offers opportunities for teachers and students to participate in discussions on current global issues, such as the effects of war on children; take part in interactive global learning projects, and exchange experiences about the use ICT in education.

Home/School Communications: Although such virtual learning communities can span the globe, they can also be formed locally. For example, in the U.S., students, parents, teachers, and administrators in the Los Angeles Unified School District's Project REBUILD have joined together into a virtual learning community with the objective of improving the performance of Limited English Proficient (LEP) students. Staff at 11 schools are using interactive videoconferencing over computer networks to jointly plan lessons and team-teach from different sites. All students in Project REBUILD schools, mostly minority children, are provided with access to the Internet and electronic mail in their classrooms and from their homes.

Homework assignments are placed on the web and informal parent-teacher conferences take place electronically whenever necessary. Staff members at the school sites receive continuing professional development instruction and consultation via videoconferencing from staff at the Center for Language Minority Education and Research at California State University Long Beach. Among other reported benefits, students in the programme have made substantial gains in English reading proficiency.

In the United Kingdom, Microsoft, Comtel and International Computers Limited (ICL) have funded the Highdown Information Hub which connects homes and schools via the Internet. Parents are able to send email to their children at school during the working day, view projects that their children are working on, and electronically converse with teachers, opening up new learning opportunities by enabling close collaboration between parents, students, and teachers.

Extending educational programmes

ICT makes it possible to extend the reach of educational programmes in two important ways. First, ICT makes it possible to deliver educational programmes anywhere in the world. Second, ICT also can help individuals learn throughout their lifetime.

Distance education programmes: Distance education programmes, also known as "distributed" education programmes, are those in which the teacher and students are physically separated, and teaching and learning takes place by means of single technologies or combinations of ICTs. In the past, such programmes made use of print, radio, and television. Now, new ICTs are driving changes in these traditional "open" or distance education programmes. Such programmes are increasing using the Internet and the World Wide Web for the delivery of courses.

For example, the International Francophone Consortium of Distance and Open Learning Institutions (CIFFAD), a consortium of open and distance learning institutions spread over 49 countries, of which 80% are in developing nations, has recently entered into a phase of reengineering to make use of new ICTs. The group aims to provide at least one hundred access points to the Internet per year in member establishments with the major part of the consortium having access to the network by the end of 1998. In an initiative making use of a combination of virtual and traditional educational programmes, Singapore's two leading research universities—the National University of Singapore and Nanyang Technological University—and The Massachusetts Institute of Technology in the U.S. recently signed an agreement to "create a new global model for long-distance engineering education and research".

The jointly developed degree programmes will enrol their first students in July 1999, and will be created and delivered by instructors from the three institutions, using a combination of faculty and student exchanges and state-of-the-art communications technology. Typically, distance education courses have been offered as supplementary programmes by campus-based educational institutions. Now, however, digital ICTs have stimulated the creation of "virtual" non-profit and for-profit educational institutions that exist partially or only in "cyberspace" and whose programmes are offered entirely by means of ICT.

Such efforts are making it possible for ICT-equipped individuals located anywhere to participate in educational programmes. The Western Governors University is an example of a "virtual university," a university that has no physical campus. WGU, initiated in 1996 by the governors of 18 of the Western United States, is a competency-based, degree-granting, virtual university: "a 'cyber' university that is not bound by its location because it doesn't have a campus in the physical sense. By using the latest technology ... WGU is able to bring classes to you, regardless of where you are". WGU is currently offering more than 300 college-level distance learning courses from 30 affiliated universities and education providers.

WGU has forged international alliances with the China Internet Education Center, Tokai University in Japan, University of British Columbia in Canada. The Open University in the United Kingdom; and the Virtual University of the Monterrey Institute of Technology in Mexico to collaborate on the development and delivery of distance learning programmes. In Germany, the four Baden universities Freiburg, Karlsruhe, Mannheim and Heidelberg recently announced the establishment of that country's first virtual university. The initiative's objective is to establish individual distance learning via e-mail, ISDN or digital television.

Within the next five years, the project will receive financial support of 8.8 million marks from the state of Baden-Wuertemberg within the framework of the "Future Initiative Young Generation". In Africa, the World Bank is funding the development of the African Virtual University (AVU). This effort holds great promise for improving educational access for people on a continent where relatively few enjoy the benefits of education, let alone a tertiary education:

> Very few African countries have attained primary education for all, despite the fact that many have been independent for some thirty years. At secondary level, the record is even worse, with many African countries able to provide secondary education to only 4 or 5 per cent of the age-group. Most African countries can boast of less than 1 per cent of the relevant age-group attaining any form of tertiary education, compared to between 25 per cent and 75 per cent in industrialised countries. And those who do attain tertiary education are unlikely to specialise in science or technology.

AVU completed a pilot phase in 1996-98 and is now moving into an operational phase when it will begin delivering full-fledged undergraduate degree programmes in Science and Engineering in January 1999. The AVU's programmes will be delivered by a combination of ICT including interactive television and the Internet. The programme is developing a digital library of scientific engineering as a resource to students and teachers. Virtual educational programmes are not limited to postsecondary education. The U.S. Department of Education has funded the Virtual High School (VHS) project, a collaborative of U.S. high schools that develops and shares web-based courses.

During the 1997-98 school year, VHS offered 29 Internet-based, credit-bearing courses to about 500 students in 27 schools located in 10 states. This approach is thought to be particularly useful as many of the participating schools either have no qualified teacher or insufficient enrolment to justify individually offering some of the courses available through the collaborative. In addition to traditional institutions using ICT to enhance or create distance learning programmes, commercial companies like Sylvan Learning Systems, Inc, in the United States and the Wall Street Institute School of English in Europe are starting ICT-based for-profit distance education programmes. Although alternate and distance education providers currently make up less than 2% of the postsecondary education market, almost $2 billion dollars has been raised on Wall Street since 1996 to finance such new ventures.

3

ICT for School Curriculum

Schools had different arrangements for co-ordinating and managing the development of ICT, particularly ICT in cross-curriculum teaching. However, a high level of development in these areas will not ensure that decisions about ICT are well thought through and appropriate, but these features do provide a supportive framework for ensuring that ICT development is well-co-ordinated and that ICT and digital materials are being used effectively throughout the school.

In 2002, the DfES commissioned the National Centre for Social Research (NatCen) and Bristol University to conduct a four-year evaluation of Curriculum Online to examine educational impacts, operational effectiveness and impact on the suppliers of educational digital materials. Their findings are described below.

ICT in Primary Schools

The role of the ICT co-ordinator in all the primary schools had changed little from last year. In primary schools, ICT co-ordinators continued to hold the role as one of a number of non-teaching roles, and rarely had clearly designated time for the role. The role was typically wide ranging and could include a range of responsibilities, from helping with ICT purchasing decisions, to planning training, to troubleshooting technical problems. ICT co-ordinators in primary schools still mostly worked in isolation without the support of ICT groups and with varying levels of support from headteachers. Consequently they valued their links with external ICT cluster groups and specialist advisory LEA staff. All the primary schools had some form of formal ICT policy, including specific ICT action and development plans, and incorporated ICT-related actions in the school development plan.

These plans varied in the amount of specific detail they included, but a number of the primary schools said that their written policies covered the use of ICT in teaching across the curriculum. For example, one school had a specific written policy for teaching and learning with ICT, and use of ICT had also to be included in each subject's policy document. In another, use of ICT was an aspect of all curriculum policies. In a further school, the annual development plan included a wide range of ICT considerations, such as development of ICT facilities and ICT training for staff, as well as ways of using ICT to enhance pupils' work and support the local community.

In this case, the action plan template had been provided by an LEA consultant. There were also examples of other strategic activities in some of the primary schools. For example, one school was planning to carry out an audit of its stock of ICT and digital materials.

The schools were originally sampled to represent a range of levels of development in ICT facilities, using computer-to-pupil ratios within three bands reflecting those used in the baseline survey of schools. The schools continued to exhibit a wide range of development of ICT facilities, with primary schools less developed overall than secondary schools. All the primary schools had PCs in classrooms, and the teachers had laptops provided through the Laptops for Teachers scheme. All the schools also had at least a couple of interactive whiteboards, but—with one exception where there was an interactive whiteboard in nearly every classroom—these were frequently shared between classes.

For some teachers, therefore, using an interactive whiteboard involved either relocating pupils into other classrooms or setting up a portable interactive whiteboard. Two primary schools had an ICT suite, but two schools did not currently have one. Of the schools without an ICT suite, one was in the process of building one, and the other school hoped to build one in the future. This school, in the meantime, was making occasional use of the ICT suite at a nearby secondary school.

However, the school did this infrequently because of the disruption involved in transporting pupils to the other school. Over the course of the year, there had been an increase in the level of ICT facilities in all the primary schools, including network developments, the purchase of interactive whiteboards, the development of ICT suites, and the purchase of small ICT items such as digital cameras. Proportionate to the level of provision last year, the increase in ICT facilities was probably a more significant development for primary schools than for secondary schools.

Technical Support in Primary Schools

Primary schools tended to use bought-in technical support, as they had last year, from the local LEA or private companies. These technicians provided varied levels of support ranging from basic troubleshooting to, in one case, the technician spending time with teachers showing them how to use equipment, in addition to solving technical problems. One school also employed a part-time technician directly, and some schools also relied on calling out someone from the manufacturer where equipment, such as interactive whiteboards, was still under warranty. Respondents were generally happy with the quality and level of technical support. The example below describes the technical support arrangements of one school that bought its support in from the LEA.

Training Opportunities

Arrangements for support and training in ICT varied across schools. Some training in primary schools was provided externally, for example, through LEAs, the National Grid for Learning (NGfL) and the New Opportunities Fund (NOF). External courses covered a range of ICT training needs, but were often focused on specific software, such as some of the crosscurricular software that was common in the primary schools.

Teachers in one school also spoke of a DfES-funded training programme, referred to as 'innovations', which, rather than focusing just on ICT skills, focused on how to use ICT to inspire and promote pupils' learning. Teachers were generally satisfied with the quality of external training although, as with last year, a couple of teachers who had undertaken NOF training said that it was too basic. Training was also frequently provided by the ICT co-ordinator or other teachers in the school, where they were familiar with specific software packages or equipment. This training would take place during staff meetings and Inset days.

For example, the ICT co-ordinator in one primary school had run an Inset day recently to introduce staff to newly purchased digital materials and online resources. Another teacher said that she thought she would find it useful to watch other teachers teaching using digital materials in the ICT suite. Some teachers said they preferred learning from colleagues in this way to attending external training courses, because it was more informal, better pitched at their needs and usually more timely.

Teachers also sometimes took software home to familiarise themselves with it. In one school, however, a teacher commented that the ICT co-ordinator had suggested that they take software home, but many of the teachers did not do so because they did not feel that they had the time. In one school, Inset days were put aside for staff to spend time exploring digital materials, hence enabling staff to familiarise themselves with software in working hours, with colleagues, and with support and assistance to hand. Many teachers also gained skills and knowledge about ICT through informal means.

Primary school teachers talked about chatting to colleagues in lunch breaks or discussing digital materials with colleagues in other schools. One primary school teacher even talked about getting help with ICT from pupils. She said that, initially, many of the teachers had been uncomfortable with this, but were now happier to ask a pupil for help. In primary schools, the level of ICT skills that classroom assistants have also continued to be a concern, although there had been some improvements since last year. For example, one primary school had arranged for classroom assistants to receive ICT training so that they could help pupils on the computer while the teacher managed the rest of the class in other activities.

One primary school also had a highly skilled special assistant who came in especially to work with the children on the computers. Overall, there seemed to be more focus on planning staff training in primary schools this year than last year. One ICT co-ordinator, for example, had included training in the ICT action plan and had developed programmes of training at three different levels of skill. In another school, ICT was a priority on the school development plan and there were actions to ensure that there were plenty of opportunities for staff to refresh and update their skills on an ongoing basis.

There was also a greater focus than last year on sharing good practice and skills between school staff, during staff meetings and Inset days. This may suggest that a core number of staff have moved past acquiring basic skills. However, the organisation and delivery of training within a school can place a lot of demands on ICT co-ordinators. For example, one ICT co-ordinator thought that her headteacher did not realise how demanding the role was. In another school, where the ICT co-ordinator was also a full-time class teacher, steps were being taken to allocate the role to someone without a full-time teaching load.

ICT in Secondary Schools

In secondary schools, the role of the ICT co-ordinator varied from school to school, as it had done in the previous year. ICT co-ordinators in some schools had designated time for the role and had strategic support from senior management and specially convened ICT groups. Others were expected to fulfil their duties in general non-contact time and had little senior support. In one case the ICT co-ordinator was not involved in many

ICT-related decisions, which were taken by the headteacher alone. Policies for ICT development in secondary schools ranged from formal written documents that were part of a formal ICT strategy to informal shared understandings.

For example, two schools claimed to have no specific written school policy covering ICT, and, in one school with specialist ICT status, decisionmaking was described as "pretty informal". In this case, teachers spoke of several people being in charge, and one teacher felt that there were "too many ICT chiefs". There was also a concern voiced by several teachers that, although the specialist ICT status had brought additional funds and had prompted the acquisition of a lot of new resources, ICT development was being driven by technicians rather than by the needs of teachers or pupils.

Other schools had written ICT policies—in one case, containing specific reference to cross-curricular use of ICT. This school had a formal strategy for ICT, and each department was directed to include use of ICT in teaching in its departmental strategies and in schemes of work.

All the secondary schools had acquired laptops through the Laptops for Teachers scheme, although one school had recently had 60 of its laptops stolen, which it had been hoping to replace in the near future. There were interactive whiteboards in most or all departments. All schools had at least one ICT suite, and several had multiple ICT suites. The more developed schools were also more likely to have a range of other ICT equipment such as laptops for pupils to use, webcams and digital cameras. One school also had plasma screens around the school for publicising and sharing information. There was sometimes variation in the level of ICT facilities between secondary school departments. This variation was due to different subject departments having had different levels of access to ICT funding in the past, because of specialist status or by other means.

For example, one school's history department had acquired special funding in the past to establish an internet café. The examples below describe the ICT facilities in two secondary schools. Over the course of the year there had been an increase in the level of ICT facilities, especially the number of interactive whiteboards, in all the secondary schools, with many schools aiming to have an interactive whiteboard in each classroom at some point in the future. Improvements in ICT facilities also included the development of additional ICT suites, networking developments, and the purchase of small ICT items such as digital cameras.

Technical Support in Secondary Schools

Some secondary schools had employed ICT technicians within the school. However, in some of the other schools, there were a number of perceived problems with technical support. In one school with a full-time technician and an assistant, there was a feeling that, although the technical staff were generally skilled and helpful, there were not enough of them and they could not always fix problems when needed. One teacher at this school was concerned about increasing the amount of ICT equipment in classrooms, because of the additional technical support needs this was likely to generate.

In another school there was a widespread feeling that the technical team were unresponsive to teachers' needs, and teachers described long delays and unhelpful approaches to solving ICT problems. These included not being able to access help to connect printers and scanners or troubleshoot problems, feeling unreasonably blamed by technicians for problems that occurred with ICT equipment (one teacher said a technician told her that "you must have turned it on wrong") and, in one case, a teacher reported that she had been waiting for over two months to have a software package loaded on to the network. Where technical problems occurred that could not be quickly remedied, for whatever reason, this could be extremely disruptive and have an impact on confidence in using ICT, even after the problem had been solved.

For example, in one school an electronic system for keeping the register and storing grades and other information kept crashing. Over the course of several terms, teachers became very stressed and frustrated. They eventually reverted to using paper or an Excel spreadsheet to record grades. Also, it took a long time to log on to. Hence, when pupils arrived late into class, teachers often did not bother logging on to the system again to register them. In another school, a large number of laptops were stolen.

Some teachers lost their work, which had been stored on the laptop without taking a backup, and this had made them reluctant to use laptops to prepare work in the future. Also, where ICT equipment or materials failed, teachers described feeling unprepared to teach. Pupils described examples of where ICT had failed to work and, as a result, teachers had taught something other than the planned topic. Some respondents thought that older teachers were better able to resort to textbooks and talking in these instances.

Training Opportunities

In secondary schools, training opportunities varied from

school to school. In some schools, the difficulties of freeing teachers from their teaching duties, and the limited number of Inset days available, led to a lot of ICT training being conducted in teachers' own time. Often this involved teachers teaching themselves at home with the help of an instruction manual. Sometimes teachers also reported having organised formal training for themselves, independently of their schools. There was a view among some teachers that there was a lack of funding for training.

One teacher, for example, thought that not enough was spent on training or support, because the money was being spent on hardware instead. In other schools training seemed to be plentiful and readily available. In one of the more developed schools, a teacher said that training was always there when it was needed, and that teachers were actively encouraged to undertake both internal and external training. In several schools, respondents said that teachers who had previously been reluctant to use ICT had become more confident.

For example, one teacher said that her ICT co-ordinator had actively, and with some success, encouraged those who were "petrified" of ICT to undertake training. Other respondents said that teachers who were previously nervous about using ICT were willing to undertake training once they had acquired new equipment in their classrooms, such as interactive whiteboards. In most schools, ICT co-ordinators ran Inset days. In one school, teachers were given formal responsibility for getting themselves training on some aspect of ICT and then cascading this to other teachers. In several schools, internal training sessions were sometimes held during school hours rather than on Inset days.

In these cases, teachers could not always attend because of timetable pressures. Attendance at such sessions was voluntary. In one secondary school, for example, lunchtime training on using the interactive whiteboards was provided only to those who signed up for it. This allowed teachers—such as newly qualified teachers—who were more skilled, to choose not to attend. However, it could mean that teachers who were either unable or reluctant to attend missed out on useful training. Teachers also described a range of external training courses, often on specific software packages.

Teachers described a number of barriers to training being effective. In one school, technical problems and a lack of effective technical support led a teacher to complain that although there were quite a lot of Inset training days, there were never enough, and she thought a major failing was that the courses did not tell you what to do when things went wrong. Technical support issues, such as programmes crashing and unresponsive technical staff, could prevent teachers from gaining confidence in using ICT, despite receiving appropriate training.

In one school, training on interactive whiteboards was provided before teachers had regular access to them, and so was never consolidated with subsequent use and practice. Indeed, regular use of digital materials was often cited as the best way of learning how to use a software program or piece of ICT equipment, and teachers frequently spoke of taking software home on their laptops to practise with, both where they had received prior formal training and where they had not. Informal means of gaining skills and knowledge were as common in secondary schools as they were in primary schools.

In one school, teachers said that they did not even know where they would go to get formal training, and relied on teaching themselves or on learning from colleagues. Another teacher said that she often helped out colleagues with databases. Informal support, however, was not always effective. Some teachers also spoke of technical staff showing them how to use digital materials. And, in one school, technicians had posted up instructions on how to use the digital camcorder and how to print pictures from it, which teachers had found useful.

A number of teachers talked about training and support for using ICT in teaching, as well as training in how to use individual software packages. One ICT co-ordinator in a secondary school said that he thought training ought to be focused differently, so that instead of being trained on specific pieces of software, teachers should be shown ideas for different ways of using ICT to teach particular principles or topics. Several teachers spoke of opportunities for sharing good practice at staff meetings.

eLearning Credits (eLCs)

eLearning Credits (eLCs) are funds set aside by the Government for schools to spend on digital materials, and are a key component of the Curriculum Online programme. Awareness and understanding of eLCs among the sample was varied. Some teachers said they had heard about eLCs, but did not really know what they were. In other cases, teachers had a basic understanding—for instance, knowing that eLCs are funding for digital materials, but knowing little more than this.

Other teachers had a more comprehensive understanding of what eLCs were—for example, knowing that they are funding for digital materials, or knowing about eLC accreditation, or sometimes knowing the amount that had been allocated to their schools. The way in which levels of awareness and understanding varied was heavily influenced by how involved respondents were in the spending of eLCs. Thus, ICT co-ordinators and senior staff, such as headteachers, were generally more knowledgeable about eLCs.

Other respondents, including department heads and subject or key stage co-ordinators, tended to know more about eLCs only if they had been directly involved in spending eLC allocations. This was broadly consistent with last year's findings. As with last year, the most widely known fact about eLCs was that they were dedicated funding for digital materials. For example, a secondary school ICT co-ordinator remarked that eLCs were for "software that's linked to learning". Other teachers referred to the eLC accreditation symbol and knew that eLCs could be spent only on materials with this accreditation.

Some teachers were also aware of certain materials being excluded from eLC accreditation, such as certain types of professional software. However, a small number of respondents were unclear about what eLCs could be spent on. Other teachers had misunderstood what eLCs were for. For example, one secondary school teacher talked about eLCs being used to pay for ICT in general, rather than digital materials specifically. Another secondary school teacher thought that the credits were specifically for buying software to accompany textbooks.

Other teachers displayed a more comprehensive understanding of eLCs, and tended to know more about the amounts allocated and the operation of the eLC funding scheme. Those who knew how much money had been allocated to the school through eLCs tended to be

ICT co-ordinators specifically, rather than teachers more generally, unless they had been directly involved in spending the eLCs.

One secondary school teacher talked about the level of funding being "in the thousands". Another secondary school teacher recalled that the eLC funding had been £16,000 two years ago. Some other teachers were able to remember how much they had been allocated as individuals or departments previously. A primary school teacher, for example, said that she had been allocated £250 of eLCs to spend in the previous year. Some respondents knew about the operation of the funding scheme.

A secondary school teacher, for example, referred to the formula for calculating schools' allocations of eLCs, explaining that it was based on the number of children in the school. A primary school teacher remarked that it was necessary to spend the eLC allocation within the year, because otherwise it would be lost. However, teachers' understand about the funding scheme was not always correct, as in the case of a primary school ICT co-ordinator who believed that eLC funding would not be available next year. As with last year, it was more common for teachers to have learnt about eLCs informally, through discussions with colleagues or software sales representatives, through suppliers' catalogues and other marketing materials, and on ICT training courses, rather than through formal communications within their schools.

However, some respondents did recall having been told about eLCs informally by their ICT co-ordinators. Overall, there did seem to have been some increase in teachers' awareness and understanding of eLCs since last year. A secondary school science teacher, for example, was aware of eLCs this year, but had not been when interviewed last year. It appeared that he had become aware of eLCs as a result of his department having used them to fund some new software that he was now using, rather than through any direct involvement in their spending.

Others had become aware of eLCs where there had been changes in the arrangements schools had for spending their allocated eLCs. For example, a secondary school history teacher had not been aware of eLCs last year, because they had been spent almost entirely on the school's maths department. This year, however, he had been approached by his ICT co-ordinator and asked what resources he would like to buy using the school's eLC funding. Other teachers were also made aware of eLCs through being consulted about how to spend them.

It is also possible that the conduct of last year's interviews themselves had an impact on teachers' knowledge and understanding of eLCs, and in one case a teacher had found out about eLCs by having a conversation with her ICT co-ordinator in preparation for the research interview.

Many respondents said that they found it easy to identify whether they could use eLCs or not when choosing digital materials. Catalogues, which were a widely used source for selecting software, were said to clearly highlight whether digital materials were accredited or not through the use of the accreditation symbol. These catalogues were either sent directly to teachers by suppliers, or had been passed on by ICT co-ordinators.

Those who were less experienced at choosing digital materials said that they always felt they could ask the ICT co-ordinator for advice on eLC accreditation. However, there was no evidence of respondents having verified whether a resource could be bought with eLCs through ICT co-ordinators. ICT co-ordinators sometimes talked about how teachers could check eLC accreditation by using the Curriculum Online website, but no teacher said that they had done this.

As with last year, there were few reports of people not being able to buy what they needed with eLCs, and most teachers said they were very happy with the range of digital materials with eLC accreditation. There were a small number of exceptions to this. Basic Microsoft packages and a professional graphic design package were examples of materials that could not be purchased with eLCs, although one teacher said that he had been able to buy a different graphic design package with eLCs.

Last year's research also highlighted the case of a secondary school teacher who said that online subscriptions to access legal and historical source materials were not covered by eLCs. In this year's interview, he talked about continuing to pay for the subscriptions out of his department's general budget. Another respondent said that there were products from smaller publishers that were excluded.

No-one who had selected digital materials said that they had been directed by an ICT co-ordinator specifically to eLC-accredited materials. This suggests that most relevant digital materials were eLC accredited and that there was no need for ICT co-ordinators to guide teachers in this way. This does not suggest that the low level of awareness of eLCs among many teachers was a barrier to them selecting accredited digital materials. Many teachers were unable to say whether digital materials had been purchased with eLCs or not. In general they assumed they had, but said that the funding source was not a concern, because they had been able to buy the digital materials they wanted.

Respondents appreciated the fact that eLCs were ring-fenced, because this had ensured that money had been invested in an area that had attracted little significant funding in the past. Some teachers commented on how eLCs should be able to be used to fund the cover needed to allow teachers time to familiarise themselves with new digital materials. This year, although no-one explicitly said that the costs of teaching cover should come out of eLC funding, several teachers said that there was still a need for teachers to have designated non-contact days for familiarising themselves with digital materials.

Overall, eLC funding tended to be seen as more than adequate for schools' needs. Some respondents also thought that, in principle, they could rely on other funding sources if they could not get the digital materials they wanted with eLCs. For example, some schools described having an ICT budget (typically mainstream funding) from which technical support and ICT maintenance costs were usually funded, but which could be used to pay for digital materials if necessary. Subject budgets and literacy and numeracy budgets were also mentioned as other means of funding purchases of digital materials.

And schools with specialist status funding talked about how some of these funds could be made available for digital materials too. However, in practice, there was little evidence of people needing to use these alternative sources of funding, and, where they did, it tended to be for relatively small purchases, such as for a CD-ROM that accompanied a textbook. Other respondents remarked on how other sources of funding for digital materials were usually limited, and how any purchase using this money would need to be strongly argued for against other spending priorities.

A variety of funding sources were referred to for spending on ICT facilities, including the National Grid for Learning (NGfL), the Standards Fund, the Laptops for Teachers initiative, the Tools for Schools scheme, specialist status funding, PTA fundraising and Tesco's Computers for Schools vouchers.

Purchasing Digital Materials

Primary schools

Digital materials were selected either by the ICT co-ordinator alone, or there was a mixed approach, with the ICT coordinator (sometimes with the headteacher) selecting some resources, with the remaining credits being allocated to groups of subjects, or with teachers being invited to submit a request to the ICT coordinator. In the one school where ICT resources were selected centrally, the ICT co-ordinator, in consultation with her ICT support assistant, decided to use this year's eLC allocation to update existing software and purchase software for new interactive whiteboards, which had been introduced into some of the younger classes. This was a somewhat different approach to that of the previous year, when she had spent part of the money on some generic software for the whole school, but shared the rest between class teachers, allocating each teacher £200.

The other three schools employed a mixed approach. In one of these, the headteacher in conjunction with the ICT co-ordinator spent a proportion of the school's eLCs on the ongoing subscription costs of a cross-curricular software package, and the remainder of the money was designated to groups of subjects. In the other two schools, the ICT co-ordinators had spent a large proportion of the school's eLCs on cross-curricular digital materials, and the remaining money was shared across the school. However, rather than allocate the money to individuals or subjects, teachers were invited to make requests for the digital materials they wanted. In both cases, this was a change from how spending had been organised in the previous year. Last year, ICT co-ordinators had spent all the eLC funding on crosscurricular resources, leaving no money to spend elsewhere.

However, this year the ICT co-ordinators found themselves with more money left over after paying ongoing subscription costs for the crosscurricular resources, and were keen to involve teachers in spending it. This approach, however, was not always successful, In one school, for example, the ICT co-ordinator ended up selecting additional digital materials herself, because only two teachers made requests. She assumed that the other teachers had been too busy to spend time looking at digital materials. ICT co-ordinators in each of the four schools were also beginning to think about how to spend next year's allocation of eLCs.

One ICT co-ordinator, for example, had done an audit of her school's digital materials, and had concluded that it had sufficient materials for its current needs, therefore she did not plan to buy any more next year. An ICT co-ordinator in another school discussed how she wanted to take stock of the resources they already had, and ensure that teachers were familiar with using them, before deciding to buy any more digital materials. The other two schools were planning quite significant changes to their premises, which were likely to have an impact on ICT developments. One school was having an ICT suite built, and expected to have to use eLC funds on site licences to cover the additional computers. The other school was due to be completely rebuilt in the near future, hopefully to include an ICT suite, and respondents in the school expected to have to review their ICT needs as a result.

Secondary schools

The same three broad approaches to eLC spending were evident in secondary schools as were found in primary schools. Hence, one of the following approaches was taken: eLCs were allocated centrally by ICT co-ordinators or headteachers to specific subject areas; teachers across the school were invited to make requests for the digital materials they wanted to purchase, and efforts were made to distribute funds evenly across a wide range of subject areas; or each department received an allocation of eLCs to spend as it wanted. Two schools employed a centralised approach. In one, the headteacher decided which subjects to spend eLCs on.

Some teachers did make direct requests to the headteacher for funds, but these requests were the result of being encouraged by the ICT co-ordinator (who had no say in how eLCs were spent), rather than in response to an open invitation. This ICT co-ordinator, when interviewed the previous year, said that the headteacher would agree to requests from teachers only where they could guarantee an impact on teaching or learning. According to the same respondent, the reason behind the headteacher managing eLC spending was because "he's just one of these people that likes to be in control of everything", and the ICT co-ordinator and teachers were not able to articulate a clear strategic purpose to this way of organising eLC spending.

In the other school where a centralised approach was taken, the ICT co-ordinator directed eLC spending to certain subject areas only. He explained that he thought it was more effective to target a smaller number of subject areas. He felt that this was the only way to introduce an adequate level of materials to link ICT to units of learning and to ensure that all pupils had the same level of access to ICT within a given subject area. He thought that if he allowed all teachers to make requests, it would most likely be the teachers with a personal interest in ICT who would make requests, and this would mean that some pupils would have more access than others to ICT in their lessons. This approach had not changed since the previous year's interview, except for the subject areas targeted.

Last year the ICT co-ordinator had spent almost all of the school's eLCs on maths, because the school had just been awarded specialist status in this subject along with ICT. This year he had decided to target what he considered to be the core subjects of English, science, maths and ICT, with a greater emphasis on English and science, because they had been neglected the year before. In two schools, teachers and heads of department were invited to make requests for the digital materials they wanted. Although departments were not allocated budgets, ICT co-ordinators were keen to ensure that eLCs were shared across the departments.

In one of the schools, where teachers could make requests all year round, the ICT co-ordinator described his school's approach as "first come first served". However, he would ensure that money was set aside for those departments that were slower to make bids, and would sometimes make active suggestions about digital materials. This approach was similar to that taken the previous year. The other school accepted requests only at set times during the year, in order to assess all requests together. Also, any digital materials purchased had to be able to be used by more than one department, so that as many pupils as possible could benefit from them. In the previous year, each department had been given its own allocation to spend.

The ICT co-ordinator said that some departments had wanted to spend beyond their budgets, whereas others had under-spent, which had meant he had had to reallocate funds between departments, and this had been time-consuming. By moving to a request system, he could allocate eLCs without having to spend time reallocating individual departments' budgets. In the final school, each department was given its own allocated budget, although choices still had to be approved by the ICT co-ordinator and network manager. This approach had not changed since last year. Compared to primary schools, there was less explicit discussion among secondary school respondents about potential arrangements for spending eLCs next year.

In one case, it was not possible to speak with the headteacher who had determined the way in which eLCs were spent without consultation or significant involvement from his ICT co-ordinator, and so were unable to find out his plans for the following year. The ICT co-ordinator in the school with departmental budgets said that she wanted to carry out an audit of what they already had and wanted to ensure it was all being used before she thought about how they should spend next year's eLCs. All the other ICT coordinators said that they did not predict any fundamental change in how they would allocate eLCs next year.

All primary school respondents said they were content with how eLC spending had been organised in their schools over the past year. However, opinions were more varied among secondary school respondents. In both primary and secondary schools, where respondents were content with the arrangements in their schools for spending eLCs, the key reason for this was that they were able to buy the resources they wanted. Some other teachers, again in both primary and secondary schools, appreciated how the spending process was organised. This included teachers both in schools with more devolved and more centralised approaches.

Some preferred a more devolved approach because it allowed them to be more involved in the selection process and to choose digital materials that suited their needs. Others preferred it when somebody else decided what digital materials were most appropriate, especially if they were unconfident in using ICT or felt they had little time to spend choosing materials themselves. Some secondary school teachers were critical of the arrangements in their schools for spending eLCs. A secondary school teacher, for example, criticised her school's approach for its lack of transparency. She also complained that she found it difficult to make choices about what to request for her department, because she had no idea how much she had to spend, and would have preferred a system where she was allocated a budget.

This secondary school teacher also felt that the lack of transparency meant that there was little coordination with regard to what was actually bought. She gave an example of how two different departments had bought the same piece of software, because they were unaware of what each other was doing. In another example, a teacher in a secondary school where bids were accepted only at a particular time of year complained that she often felt rushed by the deadline, and often unable to make well informed decisions about what digital materials to request. In yet another secondary school, a teacher complained that her request for a piece of language software had been turned down, because the software could not be used by more than one department, and so did not satisfy her school's criteria for choosing digital materials.

Respondents discussed a range of criteria that they used when selecting digital materials. Overall, these were similar to those discussed last year. However, schools and teachers varied in how well thought out their purchases seemed to be. So, for example, in some cases teachers spoke very vaguely about the kinds of criteria they used to select digital materials. In contrast, others had very explicit and clear approaches to selecting materials. For example, in one primary school the ICT coordinator had carried out an audit of digital materials in the school to identify gaps, and checked that materials were QCA-compatible, and pupils also regularly piloted new digital materials to assess user-friendliness and other features.

Some teachers spoke of the need for materials to fit with QCA and National Curriculum requirements. Others said it was important for materials to fit exactly with what was being taught and with specific schemes of work. Many teachers, consequently, valued being able to adapt digital materials to make them more appropriate to specific lessons. Others spoke about filling gaps. For example, a primary school teacher sought to expand digital materials for the computers in her classroom from primarily numeracy and literacy materials to materials to cover a wider range of subjects.

Some respondents said that materials needed to be used across different departments or subject areas and different ability levels, to benefit as many pupils as possible, and provide value for money. Primary schools had often invested in cross-curricular resources for this reason. In one secondary school, teachers were not allowed to purchase materials that served only one department, although this had led to language staff not being able to purchase any digital materials for their teaching.

Many teachers referred to the need for digital materials to be user-friendly for both teachers and pupils. Teachers wanted to be able to learn how to use the materials quickly, and not to have to keep referring to a manual. They also wanted pupils to be able to use the materials without the need for significant levels of support from teachers, so that pupils could work and learn independently.

A number of teachers said they needed materials that would be useful for all ability groups, from special educational needs, through low to moderate ability pupils, to high achievers. Teachers sometimes talked about specialist software for special educational needs. Others talked about low and high ability pupils being able to use the same digital materials, but being able to work at different levels. This was seen as ideal, and one teacher said it removed the stigma, experienced by lower ability pupils, of being given easier work. Some teachers said that one reason why some materials fell out of use was because they were not suitable for certain abilities, and pupils spoke of some programs being too easy for them.

Teachers frequently referred to the need for materials to be engaging. Teachers referred to interactivity, colours and sounds as helping to engage pupils, and a couple of respondents said that programmes that gave affirmations such as 'well done' could increase pupils' engagement.

A number of teachers said that digital materials needed to have a clear educational intent and not just be entertainment for pupils. Although no teacher spoke of buying digital materials for the prime purpose of entertainment, there were examples of teachers using digital materials for educational purposes, but also sometimes as a "treat" or to give pupils a break. Several teachers said that it was important that digital materials enhanced teaching, adding value rather than substituting or replicating what the teacher could do using other means.

Ideally digital materials should present ideas and concepts in ways that were not otherwise possible, thus providing pupils with new ways to understand and learn, and appealing to different learning styles. Teachers often said that they would generally see if they could find something suitable that was free on the internet before they considered purchasing materials. This was more relevant to certain types of materials such as lesson plans, information and pictures, quizzes and exercises, and source materials such as law reports.

A number of purchases involved updating existing digital materials or sustaining subscriptions to cross-curricular resources. There was also a need to buy digital materials for interactive whiteboards where teachers had acquired interactive whiteboards in their classrooms for the first time.

Types of Digital Materials

The study explored with teachers what digital materials

they had bought with eLCs and other funding over the last year and, more widely, the kinds of digital materials used in teaching. Within primary schools and within secondary schools there were no notable differences in the kinds of materials purchased, other than some schools focusing more on selecting digital materials for facilities such as interactive whiteboards where these were newly acquired. There were, however, some key differences between primary and secondary schools, as shown in Table 1.

Primary schools focused more on whole-school resources, safe and filtered internet-style access, and digital materials for supporting literacy and numeracy. Secondary schools used more standard Microsoft packages and professional software, there was more use of information from the internet, greater use of PowerPoint presentations and other materials that teachers had adapted themselves, and occasional use of original source materials, such as historical documents and law reports, that were not discussed at all in primary schools.

Table 1: Types of digital materials used in primary and secondary schools

Primary schools	*Secondary schools*
Focus on whole-school resources. Special focus on safe and secure internet-style searches. Specialist subject software mentioned, but strong focus on literacy and numeracy.	More use of standard Microsoft packages and professional software by pupils. More subject-specific digital materials. More use of internet and email by pupils, including subject-specific and exam revision resources on the internet.
	More focus on making own digital materials, such as

	PowerPoint presentations and quizzes and exercises.
	Use of source material such as online access to original historical and legal documents.

Sometimes teachers said that materials had fallen from use or were not used regularly. The reasons given for this were that:

- materials were faulty
- materials were not as interactive as expected
- materials were too text-based
- had found better free resources on the internet
- materials were not as easy to use as expected
- materials were not suitable for certain abilities
- there were problems with network, making it difficult to access resource
- there were delays in getting materials loaded onto school network
- there had been changes in operating system, so some packages could no longer be used
- it was not always easy to find relevant information when using cross-curricular resources
- *teachers had not had time to learn how to use the* materials.

METHODS TO FIND DIGITAL MATERIALS

Teachers used a range of different methods to find out about and access digital materials for teaching. These sources fell into three broad categories:

- internet
- suppliers' catalogues, marketing materials and ICT exhibitions
- word-of-mouth recommendations from colleagues, other teachers, trainers and advisors.

Curriculum Online Websites

Overall, awareness of the Curriculum Online website remained fairly low, and very few respondents who were aware of the site had more than a passing acquaintance with it. ICT co-ordinators were more likely than other teachers to be aware of the Curriculum Online website, with several showing a reasonable degree of familiarity with it. One of these said she used the site regularly, but did so, in part, because she felt obliged to as an ICT co-ordinator, and because she knew someone who had been involved in its design.

A number of the ICT co-ordinators recalled finding out about the Curriculum Online website through the DfES, the LEA or other external sources. Teachers, more generally, who knew about the website, tended to have found out about it either through the interviews conducted last year for this research or through ad hoc means, such as an internet search. As with last year, sometimes respondents claimed to know the website, but then did not seem to be familiar with it. For example, some respondents spoke of the website as though it were itself a crosscurricular resource, rather than being an information source and portal.

Others were unable to remember, or misremembered, many of the website's features. A number of teachers said they felt that they should use the Curriculum Online website because they knew it was associated with the eLearning Credits (eLCs), but that they had not done so. Those who said they were aware of the website; but that they did not use it or did not use it regularly, gave a range of reasons. Some said they preferred other websites, for example, Google for searching for software, and BBC or Channel 4 websites for accessing digital materials directly. They often said these websites were "more user-friendly" and valued the fact that they had free resources on them. Others preferred not to use the internet to search for digital materials at all, and preferred to rely on paper-based sources such as catalogues or word of mouth.

Those who were familiar with the Curriculum Online website registered a number of opinions. One respondent said that she thought that the website—particularly the search facility—had improved over time. Others continued to cite problems with the search facility, reporting that even tightly defined searches threw up an unmanageably large number of items. In many cases, not all the items identified seemed relevant. On the other hand, one respondent also said that the search did not locate digital materials that he knew existed and were eLC accredited.

Another teacher said she wanted "exam stuff", whereas she thought most of the materials were aimed at Key Stages 1, 2 and 3. Others found the website generally hard too use. One described it as "dull", and another respondent commented that the website came across as "politically correct" and was full of educational "buzzwords". Some respondents valued the fact that the website contained information on a wide range of materials, and that it gathered information on all eLC-accredited materials in one place. One respondent liked the fact that material was organised by key stage.

Another respondent thought that the website gave access to the cheapest means of purchasing digital materials. A number of respondents valued the free downloadable materials. However, other teachers thought that it was hard to distinguish between free and paid-for materials on the website, and that, in many cases, there were better free materials available elsewhere. One teacher wondered whether it was possible to access free trials of software through the Curriculum Online website, to see the digital materials in action. An ICT co-ordinator thought that the website lacked digital materials from some smaller publishing houses, which he thought were often excellent. Written evaluations of the digital materials were appreciated, although one respondent said that the value of these was limited because little information about the context and transferability was included.

So, for example, the materials may have been used in a school with different levels of literacy or socio-economic deprivation. Another teacher noted that several of her choices of digital materials did not have teacher evaluations. Overall, these teachers thought more extensive and detailed user feedback on materials would be useful. The steering group for the study had shown an interest in how teachers felt about placing orders through the site, and also about being able to access eLC spend data. When asked about these issues, respondents generally thought that the ability to place orders via the website was a good idea, but that this would need to be restricted to a single budget-holder or named person to reduce the risk of duplicating orders. Respondents, however, generally saw little benefit in storing eLC spend data on the website, because this was available within the school.

Some teachers mentioned other specific websites, usually providing free information and materials, such as the Channel 4, BBC, Granada Learning, and the London School of Economics websites. Other teachers talked about finding information and materials through general internet searches, although sometimes search filters within schools made it difficult to search for some topics. Some teachers seemed to be adept at accessing materials using the internet, while others were unsure about where to get information from. Other than the internet, teachers used suppliers' catalogues, marketing materials and exhibitions, as well as word of mouth to identify and access digital materials for teaching.

As with last year, many teachers spoke about being "bombarded" with fliers and advertising material from suppliers of digital materials, much of which teachers said ended up in the bin. However, many teachers were cynical about the information they got from suppliers in publicity material. One secondary school teacher, for example, said she preferred to have digital materials on 14- or 30-day trial because "the blurb blows their trumpet, but you need to see it". Another teacher said that the information in fliers is often quite limited, and although he sometimes means to telephone the supplier to find out more, in practice he rarely gets around to it.

Some teachers relied on brand recognition. For example, one textiles teacher bought a software program from a supplier of sewing machines that she knew to be reliable. Catalogues remained popular sources of information about digital materials. These were sometimes ordered, but also came through the post unsolicited. They were thought to contain more information about products than fliers and other publicity materials, although one teacher said that some were more detailed than others. Unlike many other sources, they could be looked at in a range of circumstances, such as in the staff room or on the bus. One primary school teacher, for example, said that you could flick through a catalogue during a spare five minutes at lunchtime, and eat your lunch at the same time.

A secondary school teacher said that it was quicker for her to browse through a catalogue than to log on to the internet. Although catalogues were an important source of information, teachers rarely relied solely on this information to make their selections. They might, for example, discuss the digital materials they were interested in with internal and external colleagues. In one school, the network manager would carry out further research about packages that teachers had identified through catalogues. Most frequently, teachers would try to get materials demonstrated or obtain them on trial so they could see how they worked in practice. This seems to be a development from last year, when there was much more discussion of selecting software from catalogues alone.

However, not all suppliers appeared to offer demonstrations and/or trials. Some teachers described suppliers coming into the school to demonstrate digital materials, often at staff meetings. This was found by some teachers to be useful, and there were examples of teachers buying software and materials that had been demonstrated in this way. Other teachers, however, said that they did not always have the time to attend the sessions. Similarly, teachers sometimes found it difficult to find the time to try out materials. National ICT shows and exhibitions allowed teachers to view a range of different digital materials from different suppliers, have them demonstrated, and ask questions of suppliers' representatives.

One secondary school sent six teachers each year to ICT shows to learn about current digital materials, and thought this was an effective and efficient approach. Subject conferences were also a valuable source of information for a number of teachers, and had the advantage of allowing teachers scope to talk to a wide range of other teachers with experience of using specialist digital materials. However, to be able to attend a show or conference, teachers had to be taken out of school, and expensive teaching cover had to be arranged.

For some schools, this seemed to be a barrier to greater use of such events. In some cases, teachers found sales representatives at IT shows and events uninformative. For example, one secondary school language teacher said that the sales representative did not speak the foreign language in question, and so was not able to demonstrate the software very well. Another secondary school teacher said that the sales representative had "talked about money all the time" rather than explaining how the software worked and what you could do with it.

Word-of-mouth Sources

Word-of-mouth sources included recommendations from: immediate colleagues, including teachers, technical staff and specialist assistants; colleagues in other schools (such as through local networks of subject co-ordinators or cluster groups); the local LEA; and recommendations made on training courses. Teachers valued finding out about digital materials through word of mouth since it reduced the time that needed to be spent searching for information using the internet and other sources. In many cases, digital materials were recommended during activities that teachers took part in as a matter of course, such as staff meetings, meetings of cluster groups or subject co-ordinators' networks, or training courses.

However, in some cases, teachers were very proactive, and recommendations were actively sought. For example, one primary school teacher had to seek out new digital materials when she moved to a system of having pupils working in groups (including having a group on the computer), engaged in different activities on the same topic. To identify appropriate digital materials she relied heavily on seeking recommendations from a wide range of individuals such as colleagues, teachers in other schools, and the LEA advisor. The same teacher was getting an interactive whiteboard for her classroom in the coming year, and was already asking a range of contacts for recommendations for digital materials to use with it.

Another teacher in a secondary school spoke about making a point of going to other schools and talking to other people before selecting a digital resource for maths. There was a view that a recommendation meant that the materials were more likely to be easy to use and of high quality. However, recommendations were not always found to be reliable. One teacher in a primary school, for example, had bought some music software that had been recommended on a course, and had not found it as user-friendly as she had hoped. And recommendations from other teachers, especially immediate colleagues, were not always relevant to the respondent's year group. Finally, in one school, where no word-of-mouth feedback about particular digital materials was available, teachers would ensure that materials were acquired on a trial basis only.

4

ICTs and Pedagogy Technology Integration

ICT has to be infused into pedagogy in such a way that its uses improve learning. Countries in the Asia-Pacific region are at different stages of ICT development, in terms of both infrastructure and application of ICT in teaching and learning. Within any such country, there may be uneven development from region to region, area to area, and even from institution to institution. The Asia-Pacific region has a wide range of ICT development stages in education. In view of the above considerations, it is useful to have a model for ICT development for developing competency standards for teacher development.

Such a model can be a representation of the essential characteristics of ICT development to provide a scaffold or a framework. It can also be useful to show the inter-relationship of various components within a system and thus, help to locate its position in the whole framework. Models and frameworks can be useful in portraying how complex systems operate. Usually in visual form, they depict the major components in a system and the way these relate to each other. A framework for the integration of pedagogy and ICT in teacher education programmes, for instance, can show the major parts and the inter-relationship of these parts. To the extent that such a framework reflects all that occurs, it may then serve as a blueprint that curriculum developers can take as a starting point in determining content, sequencing, and pedagogical process. Based on the UNESCO publication, a model has been presented that can be useful in determining the stage of ICT development reached by a country, a district, or even an individual institution.

STAGES OF ICT DEVELOPMENTS

Studies of ICT development in both developed and developing countries identify at least four broad approaches through which educational systems and individual institutions typically proceed in their adoption and use of ICT. Sometimes, the number of stages identified varies. However, there is a general consensus that the introduction and use of ICT in education proceeds in broad stages that may be conceived as a continuum or series of steps. These steps, termed Emerging, Applying, Infusing, and Transforming, are elaborated in Figure 1.

Emerging stage: Institutions at the initial stages of ICT development demonstrate the emerging approach. Such institutions have just started their journey in the ICT field with a skeleton computing infrastructure either donated or purchased by the institution authority. To start with, administrators and teachers just begin to explore the possibilities and consequences of using ICT for institutional management and adding ICT to the curriculum.

Institutions at this emerging phase are still firmly grounded in traditional, teacher-centred practice. The curriculum reflects an increase in learning how to acquire ICT basic skills such as office automation, e-mail and basic operation of computers, so that it prepares the ground for moving to the applying stage. In the emerging approach to ICT development, the focus is on the technical functions and uses of ICT and on the need for some knowledge and representation of the impacts of ICT on the system as a whole.

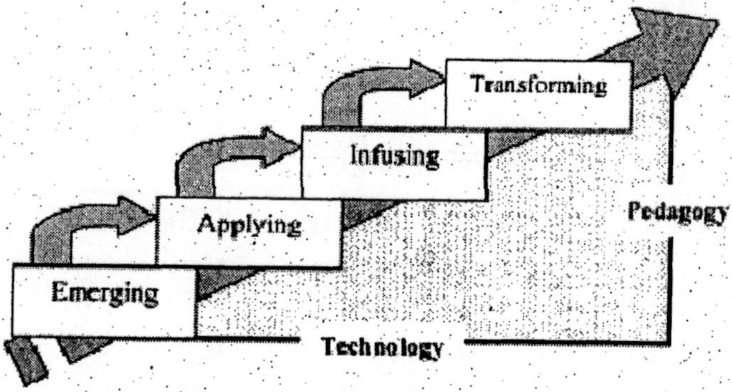

Figure 1: Stages of ICT development

This approach often involves teachers' personal use of ICT, such as, the use of word processing to prepare worksheets, locating information on CD-ROMs or on the Internet, or communicating with friends and family by e-mail. Here, teachers are developing their ICT literacy and learning how to apply ICT to a range of personal and professional tasks. The emphasis is on training in a range of tools and applications, and increasing teachers' awareness of the opportunities for applying ICT to their teaching in the future.

Applying stage: Those institutions, in which a new understanding of the contribution of ICT to learning has developed, exemplify the applying approach. In this secondary phase, administrators and teachers use ICT for *tasks already carried out in institutional management and* in the curriculum. Teachers largely dominate the learning environment. Institutions at the applying approach phase adapt the curriculum in order to increase the use of ICT in various subject areas with specific tools and software such as drawing, designing, modelling and application of specific tools. This curriculum assists movement to the next stages, if so desired.

In the applying stage, teachers use ICT for professional purposes, focusing on improving their subject teaching in order to enrich how they teach with a range of ICT applications. This stage often involves teachers in integrating ICT to acquire specific subject skills and knowledge, beginning to change their teaching methodology in the classroom, and using ICT to support their training and professional development. Teachers gain confidence in a number of generic and specialised ICT tools that can be applied to the teaching of their subject area. The opportunity to apply ICT in all their teaching is often limited only by a lack of ready access to ICT facilities and resources, which is why it is not fully integrated into all lessons for all students.

Infusing stage: At the third stage, the infusing approach involves integrating or embedding ICT across the curriculum, and is seen in those institutions that now employ a range of computer-based technologies in laboratories, classrooms, and administrative offices. Teachers explore new ways in which ICT changes their personal productivity and professional practice. The curriculum begins to merge subject areas to reflect real-world applications. In the infusing approach to ICT development, ICT infuses all aspects of teachers' professional lives in such ways as to improve student learning and the management of learning processes.

The approach supports active and creative teachers who are able to stimulate and manage the learning of students, integrating a range of preferred learning styles and uses of ICT in achieving their goals. The infusing stage often involves teachers easily integrating different knowledge and skills from other subjects into project-based curricula. In this approach, teachers fully integrate ICT in all aspects of their professional lives to improve their own learning, as well as, the learning of their students. Thus, they use ICT to manage not only the learning of their students but also their own learning. They use ICT to assist all students to assess their own learning in achieving specific personal projects. In this approach, it becomes quite natural to collaborate with other teachers in solving common problems and in sharing their teaching experiences with others.

Transforming stage: Institutions that use ICT to rethink and renew institutional organisation in creative ways are at the transforming approach. ICT becomes an integral, though invisible, part of daily personal productivity and professional practice. The focus of the curriculum is now learner-centred that integrates subject areas in real-world applications. ICT is taught as a separate subject at the professional level and is incorporated into all vocational areas. Institutions have become centres of learning for their communities.

In the transforming approach to ICT development, teachers and other staff members regard ICT as a natural part of the everyday life of the institutions that they begin to look at the process of teaching and learning in new ways. The emphasis changes from teacher-centred to learnercentred. Teachers, together with their students, expect a continuously changing teaching methodology designed to meet individual learning objectives.

Mapping the Model

The continuum model can be mapped onto two interwoven tracks for the development of teachers' capacity in harnessing ICT with regard to (a) stages of ICT usage and (b) pedagogical usages of ICT.

Different Stages of ICT Usage

Studies of teaching and learning in schools around the world identify four broad stages in the way that teachers and students learn about and gain confidence in the use of ICT. These four stages give rise to the mapping depicted in Figure 2(a) that shows the stages in terms of awareness, learning how, understanding how and when, and specialising in the use of ICT tools according to the stages of the proposed model.

Becoming aware of ICT: In the initial phase, teachers and learners become aware of ICT tools and their general functions and uses. In this stage, there is usually an emphasis on ICT literacy and basic skills. This stage of discovering ICT tools is linked with the emerging stage in ICT development.

Learning how to use ICT: Following on and from the first stage comes the stage of learning how to use ICT tools, and beginning to make use of them in different disciplines. This stage involves the use of general or particular applications of ICT, and is linked with the applying stage in the ICT development model.

Understanding how and when to use ICT: The next stage is to understand how and when to use ICT tools to achieve a particular purpose, such as in completing a given project. This stage implies the ability to recognise situations where ICT will be helpful, choosing the most appropriate tools for a particular task, and using these tools in combination to solve real problems. This stage is linked with the infusing stage in the ICT development model.

Specialising in the use of ICT: The fourth and the last stage involves specialising in the use of ICT tools which occurs when one creates and transforms the learning environment with the help of ICT. This is a new way of approaching teaching and learning situation with specialised ICT tools and is linked with the transforming stage in the ICT development model.

Pedagogical Usages of ICT

Adoption of ICT in the classroom generally proceeds in four broad stages in the way the teachers and learners use ICT as a support to teaching and learning. These four stages give rise to the mapping depicted in Figure 2(b) that have been broadly classified as supporting work performance, enhancing traditional teaching, facilitating learning and creating innovative learning environments, according to the stages of the proposed model.

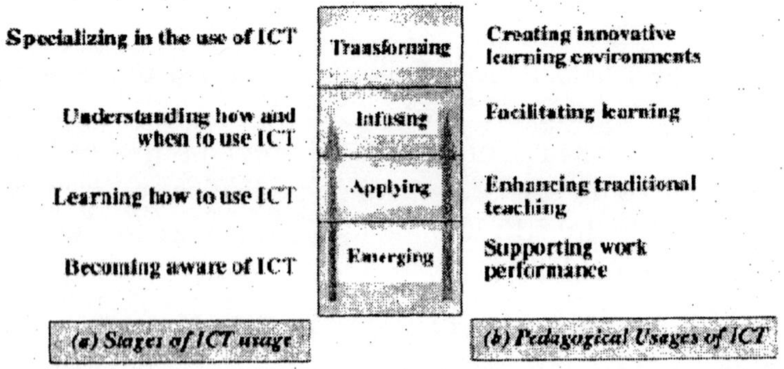

Figure 2: Mapping the Model

More than three decades ago, computers and related information technology were introduced to educators for direct teaching and learning purposes. ICT started its journey primarily with productivity tools, proceeded to self-learning courseware and multi-modal instruction, and finally progressed to web-based learning management system.

Supporting work performance: In the initial phase, teachers use productivity tools such as word processor, visual presentation software, spreadsheet, database, email etc., to support their daily work performance. During this stage, there is usually an emphasis on basic operations of electronic office software. This stage of using productivity tools for teaching and learning is linked with the emerging stage in ICT development.

Enhancing traditional teaching: Following on and from using productivity software, comes the stage of learning how to use and develop computer-assisted learning software and beginning to make use of such software in different disciplines. This stage involves the technique of integrating computer-based learning in the traditional instructional process, and is linked with the applying stage in the ICT development model. Various instructional packages were selected, developed and used to enhance traditional classroom teaching.

Facilitating learning: The next stage involves using various types of instructional software to facilitate student learning. The key point is that the teachers need to learn how to choose the most appropriate tools for a particular task, and using these tools in combination to solve real life problems. This stage implies the ability to recognise situations where various multimedia and specialised software can be utilised for teaching and learning. This stage is linked with the infusing stage in the ICT development model.

Creating innovative learning environments: The fourth and last stage involves specialising in the use of ICT to create an innovative learning environment that transforms the learning situation. This is possible by incorporating emerging trends in pedagogy and learning principles in teaching and learning. For this purpose, specialised software including modelling and simulation, expert systems, semantic networking etc., are employed to support pedagogical innovation. It helps to develop, deliver and manage open and flexible learning programme. This stage is linked with the transforming stage in the ICT continuum model.

ICT and Pedagogy

Teacher education can be represented as a continuum (Figure 3) from initial pre-service education of teachers undertaken in universities or colleges of education and extending to the induction of budding teachers and their continuing professional development in institutions.

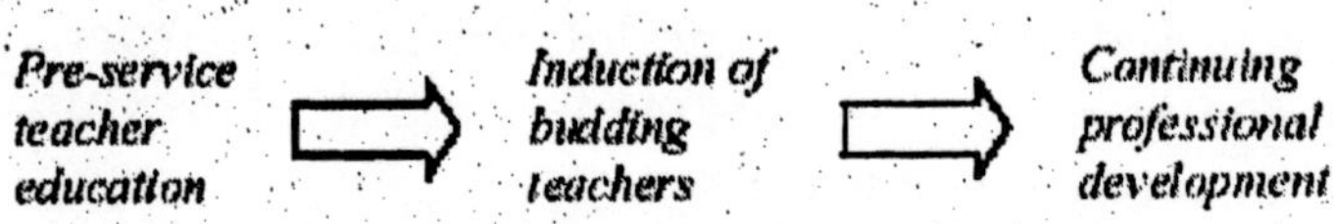

Figure 3: A continuum of professional development of teachers

Frameworks

Frameworks, like models, do not have the property of being true or false. Rather, these may be useful, more useful, or perhaps not at all useful, for particular purposes.

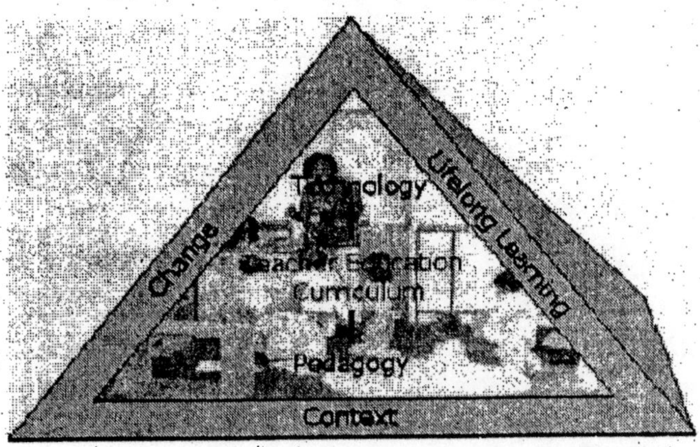

Figure 4: A curriculum framework for integrating ICT and pedagogy in professional teacher education programmes

After modification in a workshop organised by UNESCO Bangkok, this framework shows teacher competencies of pedagogy and technology operating within an environment that is characterised by change and the need to continue learning throughout life (Figure 4). The different components of the framework are considered in Figure 4.

Contextual factors

Every curriculum is a product of the environment in which it is positioned. This environment, called here contextual factors, includes three inter-related sets of factor: context, change, and lifelong learning.

Context

The most obvious contextual factor within which any teacher education curriculum is planned is context. Context has a spatial dimension, which implies that it includes all the physical or environmental conditions about which curriculum planners need to be aware of. These include such factors as the economic conditions within a country, and the quality of the telecommunications infrastructure in place. Included as well are cultural and linguistic factors that arise, for instance, in consideration of whether particular software is appropriate or not.

But context also has a temporal dimension, which implies that a particular curriculum is a product of time. As time changes, for instance, with changing political structures or demands in the workplace for new kinds of skill, the context changes. This needs to be taken into account by curriculum planners.

Change

Change, and increasingly rapid change, characterises modern societies. Driven by the revolution in ICT, new skills are required by the needs for an increasingly skilled workforce. This societal change, in turn, demands curriculum reforms in education systems around the world. It is this kind of change that the Delors Report of the International Commission on Education for the Twentyfirst Century identifies as creating tension between tradition and modernity.

Change, then, is a key contextual factor in developing teacher education curricula. Clearly, leadership and vision are essential in planning and managing change, as is consideration of key stakeholders. In developing and implementing a curriculum to integrate ICT and pedagogy in teacher education, the UNESCO Planning Guide identifies who are the key stakeholders in the different sections within which a teacher education programme operates. These stakeholders include:

- the dean or professor with responsibility for teacher education
- the teaching staff in a programme of teacher education
- senior administrators in the institution
- pre-service teachers interested *in acquiring ICT skills*
- teachers and heads of institutions organising field experiences for teachers in training
- government agencies that set policies for teacher professional development
- business and industries with an interest in the overall quality of graduates

All stakeholders need to: (a) share a common vision with respect to ICT; (b) modify the curriculum in teacher education; and (c) focus on making technology and sufficient resources available.

Lifelong learning

Lifelong learning, and indeed life-wide learning are other contextual factors since it is now recognised that learning does not stop after formal education ends. Again, the Delors Report recognised that learning throughout life is the only means to manage the tension between the extraordinary expansion of knowledge and capacity of human beings to assimilate it. The nature of ICT is one such change that curriculum planners need to build into teacher education curriculum, in order to enable budding teachers to continue their learning after graduating from the institution.

The inner core of the teacher education curriculum pyramid shown in Figure 4 comprises core teacher competencies, which are grouped into two major clusters of pedagogy and technology. These two clusters of teacher competencies, although discussed individually below, are not independent of each other in a curriculum where ICT is infused in pedagogical practice. As such, the basic philosophy of competencies of integration has also been highlighted separately.

The UNESCO Planning Guide nominates pedagogy, along with content, as "the most important aspect of infusing technology in the curriculum". Infusion of ICT begins with teachers' mastery of the content of the subjects. With incorporation of ICT in teaching, teachers develop new ways of doing things, gradually changing the focus of classroom activities from an emphasis on teaching to an emphasis on learning. At first, teachers discover ICT tools such as, presentation software. This is followed by application of ICT tools in place of previous instructional activities, such as preparing a PowerPoint presentation in place of a lecture.

As teachers become more familiar with ICT in the subjects, new ways of using ICT are explored so that their previous classroom delivery mechanism begins to change. In time, their classroom practice becomes transformed as the focus of the classroom becomes learner-centred and students use ICT to solve real-world problems that cut across traditional subject boundaries. Pedagogy includes much more. It includes theoretical knowledge and pedagogical skills. East China Normal University in Shanghai has developed a strong pre-service teacher education programme that focuses on educational uses of ICT and meaningfully integrates theory, pedagogical practice, and technology.

The key to the integrated curriculum approach at East China Normal University is, first, integrating on-campus training in ICT with field practice; second, integrating theoretical learning with pedagogical practice; and, third, integrating hands-on activities with minds-on activities—that is, learning by doing in combination with mental activities such as peer evaluation and self-reflection. Pedagogy that further engages learners in critical thinking, creative thinking and problem solving skills is the core component of ICT integration.

Whereas learning through facts, drill and practices, rules and procedures was more adaptive in earlier days, learning through projects and problems, inquiry and design, *discovery and invention, creativity and diversity, action and* reflection is more fitting now in the ICT-supported environment. Learning becomes constructivist, self-directed, flexible, interactive, deep and collaborative processing of knowledge. Collaboration and networking are other aspects of pedagogy. The real power of ICT comes from new ways of communicating beyond the four walls of the classroom and by locating information from worldwide sources wherever these may be located. The implication for teachers as they assist their students in collaborating with other learning groups and using networks to research assignment topics is that they cease to be the main source of knowledge in the classroom.

Instead, teachers' roles change from being "a sage on the stage" to becoming "a guide on the side". Teachers need to accommodate a philosophical shift in their approach to teaching. The UNESCO Planning Guide asserts that the development of teachers' competencies in collaboration and networking is essential to infusing ICT in the curriculum: Through collaboration and networking, professional teachers promote democratic learning within the classroom and draw upon expertise both locally and globally.

Advances in technology and the way technology is incorporated into a system constitute a dynamic process. Each institution has to work within the context of its own system to fit choices to what best suits its unique situation and culture. The stages can be considered as hierarchical with the emerging stage as a starting point, and the transforming stage as a goal, which many perceive as the future of education. In the emerging stage, the focus is on the basic technical functions and uses of ICT. This stage involves teachers' competencies in word processing, spreadsheet, database, presentation software and uses of Internet and e-mail.

Besides the kinds of ICT competencies relating to concepts and operations, there are many social, legal and ethical issues associated with the use of ICT about which teachers need to know. The facilities required to access information easily from remote sources, the ability to download it to a personal computer, and the utilisation of the information in a classroom assignment, brings with it a host of social, legal, and ethical issues relating to copyright, evaluation of information sources, and appropriate forms of acknowledging electronic information. In the applying stage, teachers use ICT for professional purposes, focusing on improving the teaching of subjects so as to enrich how to teach with a range of ICT tools.

In the infusing stage, teachers infuse ICT in all aspects of professional life to improve student learning and the management of learning processes. ICT enables teachers to become active and creative in stimulating and managing the learning process, by infusing a range of preferred learning styles and uses of ICT in achieving educational goals. Teachers are required to master authoring tools, animation tools and multimedia tools to develop instructional software in different subjects.

The transforming stage is linked with schools that have used ICT creatively to rethink and renew school organisation. ICT becomes an integral part of daily personal productivity and professional practice. The focus of the curriculum is now much more learner-centred and integrates subject areas in real-world applications, both in real and virtual environments. Teachers need to master special software, learning management system simulation and modelling tools, expert system, semantic networking and various web tools, in order to innovatively transform the teaching and learning system.

Although the approaches above are not a necessary hierarchical, these are intended to illustrate the steps towards growing ICT confidence and competence that many teachers go through, before beginning to transform teaching practice and the learning of their students. Bearing in mind the contextual factors of change and lifelong learning, teachers are required to be competent in using new hardware and software. Technological competencies also have an attitudinal dimension. Cabanatan emphasised the importance of a positive attitude towards ICT and a clear understanding of the potential of ICT in education.

The inclusion of both pedagogy and technology as core competencies for teachers acknowledges that integrating ICT in education for teaching and learning is far broader than the simple acquisition of these two sets of competencies. Competencies of integration are neither competencies of technology alone nor are they competencies of pedagogy. Rather competencies of integration are about the appropriate selection, use, mix, fusion and integration of many sets of competencies including those covered under pedagogy and technology. The following analogy of 'interdisciplinary thinking' illustrates (Figure 5) the spirit of integration of pedagogy and technology.

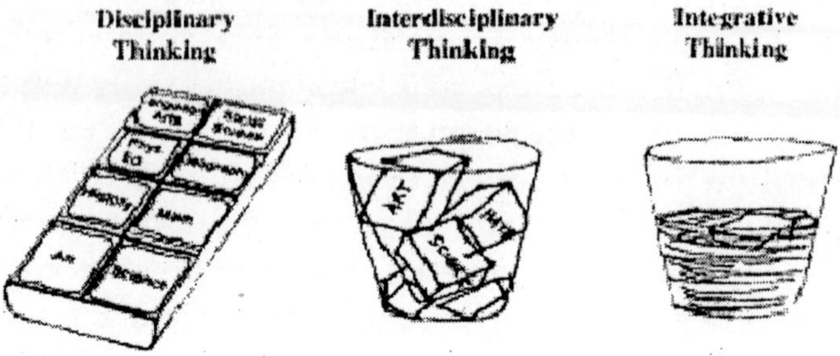

Figure 5: Interdisciplinary thinking illustrating the spirit of integration of pedagogy and technology

Having established a curriculum framework for teacher development in pedagogy-technology integration, a subsequent step is to begin the task of formulating the curriculum. As described in the UNESCO-IBE Training Guide for Curriculum Specialists, the term curriculum implies the following:

— It refers to a contract between society, the State, and educational professionals with regard to educational experiences that learners should undergo during certain phases of their lives.

— It answers the why, what, when, where, how, and with whom the learning is to take place.

— It defines the foundations and content of education, their sequencing in relation to the amount of time available for the learning experiences planned, in terms of:

  — methods to be used

  — resources for learning and teaching, such as textbooks and new technologies, and

  — evaluation.

Accordingly, pedagogy-technology integration forms an essential component of the overall curriculum for teacher education. As such, pedagogy-technology integration has to be referred to and even incorporated into the curriculum reforms for both pre-service teacher education as well as in-service teacher training in different countries of the Asia-Pacific region. In this way, all courses and subjects in teacher education/training programmes will be conducted on the basis of integrating ICT with curriculum. The expected teachers graduated from universities will, therefore, be qualified for the teaching profession in new knowledge and lifelong learning society, while in-service teachers can be continuously trained and updated.

In addition, the relationship between both curriculum reforms in basic education and teacher education need to be emphasised. This is mainly because of the current disparity between both these reforms. In some countries, curriculum reforms in basic education have gone ahead, but curriculum reforms for teacher education have lagged far behind, and this has had disadvantages for preparing tomorrow's teachers of the 21st century. The relationship between these curricula is shown in Figure 6.

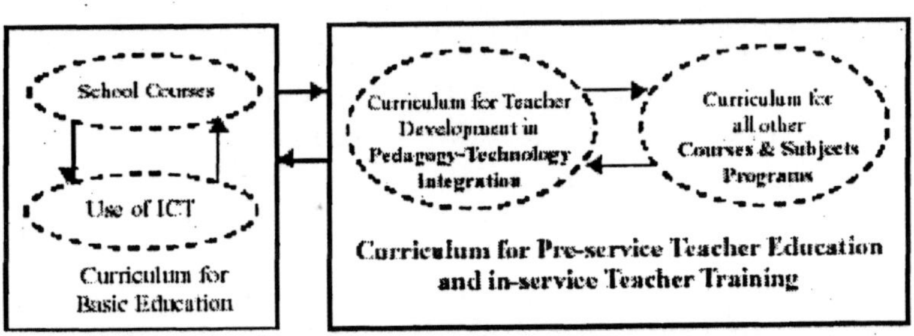

Figure 6: Close relationship of curriculum reforms in basic education and teacher education

Competency Standards

Placing pedagogical competencies at the base of the pyramid in Figure 4 reinforces the key place of pedagogy in ICT integration. This means that learning activities involving ICT have to be embedded in a real-world context, and that students engage in such activities not only because they are required, but also because they are intrinsically interesting.

It also means that an infusion of ICT, like any other learning activity, has to have clear and specific goals, and encourage learners to collaborate with one another. The competency standards recommended for teachers are not just about technical skills. It also covers pedagogical skills, integration strategies and new ways of using ICT that help students think, understand, and learn.

A competency is a set of attributes covering knowledge, skills and attitudes for enabling one to effectively perform the activities of a given occupation or function to the standards expected in employment. The notion of competence with regard to the use of ICT in education is broader than the technical skills needed to use ICT. To take a technical view of competence is to deny the plethora of skills needed by teachers to create meaningful and productive learning contexts for learners. Therefore, whilst it may be easy to take a technical view of ICT competence, this is not sufficient to equip teachers to understand, and make effective use of, ICT in the classroom.

The type of ICT competence needed by teachers is a collection of knowledge, skills and attitudes that are inextricably bound up with the context and pedagogy. Competence needs to be embedded in teacher practices. A number of countries have developed national or regional

ICT competency standards including Australia, Canada, People's Republic of China, India, New Zealand, United Kingdom and the United States. Commonly, standards are developed first to describe what students have to do with ICT at different levels of schooling.

Based on expected student outcome, a subsequent step is usually to describe what competencies their teachers are required to possess. In some cases, a further development is to create standards for educational administrators. All are particularly important to those who are responsible for providing pre-service and in-service teacher education. Competency standards can be stated either generally or quite specifically. A UNESCO publication is a useful reference here. An example of a general standard is that: Learners should be able to search the Internet. By contrast, a more specific standard is that: Learner should be able to search the Internet skilfully and intelligently to locate, evaluate, and collect information.

Relation between Standards and Curriculum Format

There is an important relationship between continuum models, curriculum frameworks and competency standards in ICT. When agreement is reached within a country or region for a curriculum framework for integrating ICT into learning, the development of competency standards for students and their teachers can follow. Furthermore, once a clear statement about ICT competency standards is arrived at, it is then possible to adapt or develop training modules for teachers. Standards do not imply a prescribed course of study for all teachers across subject areas, nations, and regions.

Generally, standards present a set of competencies that each local group of educators can interpret and translate into classroom practice based on their local context, the particular subject being taught, and their vision of ICT in education. While educators throughout the region share many common goals and beliefs about education, they come from different cultures. These cultures dictate that calls for fuller integration of ICT into education are sensitive to these cultural differences. Change will not occur in the same manner in each nation or within different locations in any one nation. Competency standards, therefore, are often closely tied to local standards for students, so that expected student outcome in a particular field of study implies a set of competencies with ICT that their teachers should possess.

From the ICT continuum model, depicted in Figure 1, competency levels can be derived that reflect a teacher's continuous development of technology capability and pedagogical capability based on a curriculum framework. Figure 7 shows how a programme of teacher development can help individual teachers move through the four stages in ICT development.

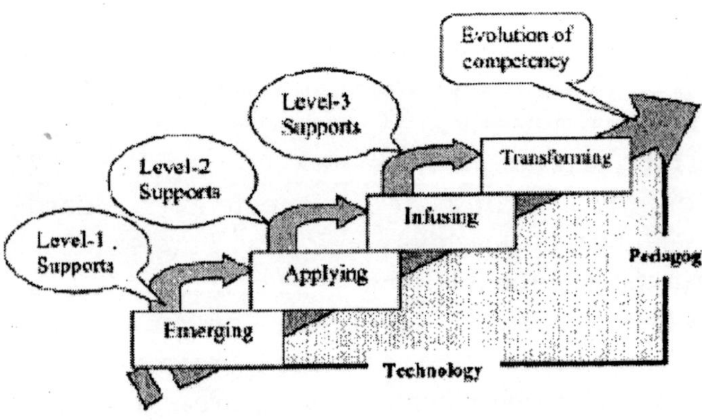

Figure 7: Points of support provided by teacher education to promote movement through the stages of ICT development

To be most effective, the ICT activities that a development programme provides are likely to deepen in complexity as a teacher's understanding and skills improve. The activities, therefore, have to be carefully designed to promote a teacher's movement into the next stage. Level-1 supports promote movement from stage 1 to stage 2, level-2 supports promote movement from stage 2 to stage 3, and level-3 supports promote movement from stage 3 to stage 4. Each stage of the ICT development model characterises the expertise the teacher is required to possess in pedagogy clusters, technology clusters and integration strategies. For example, teachers who are in the emerging stage are first becoming aware of the potential to use ICT in teaching and learning.

The development programme might provide basic support through guidance by a mentor who helps these teachers to use ICT within their subject areas in simple but important ways. This will encourage the movement of these teachers into the applying stage, in order to be engaged in more complex activities that promote deeper understanding. Here, the development programme might provide support through opportunities for discussion with colleagues doing similar work, or by providing collections of effective ICT infusions on a resource website. This encourages further growth into the infusing stage, when these teachers begin to apply knowledge and skills from other subjects into project based curricula.

In the fourth and final stage i.e., transforming stage, teachers specialise in the use of ICT tools to create an innovative learning environment. This is a completely new way of approaching teaching and learning using ICT. In this stage, various software like experts systems, semantic networking, modelling and simulation etc., can be utilised to support innovative pedagogical approach. Teachers just beginning to develop pedagogical skills are to be measured by standards represented by the emerging level of pedagogy. They progress through the standards as they further develop their skills. It is important to note that some teachers who have strong pedagogical skills and understanding may have limited skills with technology; for this, such teachers would be evaluated by the infusing standards in pedagogy, and the emerging standards in technology skills and integration strategies.

Again, the standards for integration strategies at all levels have to reflect infusions of technology that support meaningful learning. With this approach, teachers are stimulated to develop through a natural progression implied by the standards, gaining both competence and confidence as they do so. Why are such careful support strategies required? This is because teachers resist ICT innovations that do not match the context in which they work, but tend to integrate technology when it addresses real classroom problems, situations and learning goals. Teachers adapt to change when it is possible to set the goals, to have opportunities to acquire the needed skills, and to reflect on learning.

It is the desire of teachers to infuse ICT directly into students' academic lives so that student activities are authentic and meaningful from the earliest stages. A similar approaches towards teacher training needs to be adopted. Teachers are required to develop the simplest ICT skills in the midst of authentic teaching and learning activities that are seen as viable ways to solve existing professional and pedagogical problems. Teacher development is to be carefully planned, which is appropriate to a teacher's understanding and skills. This means that teachers learn to use ICT always within their zone of proximal development, so that activities are simple enough that teachers can place new ideas within the context of previous understanding, but are challenging enough to give their work meaning and purpose. Standards can play a key role in facilitating this kind of support.

Based on the continuum model and support described above, competency levels can be identified and grouped into four major clusters as shown in Table 1. These four major clusters are categorised as

- integrating productivity tools in learning context,
- enhancing teaching and facilitating learning,
- processing curriculum resources and learning materials, and
- integrating ICT for pedagogical innovations encompassing the four stages in ICT development namely, emerging, applying, infusing and transforming stages.

Table 1 further elaborates the major pedagogical and ICT skills with corresponding integration strategies required for every cluster of competency standards stated above. This analytical framework of competency standards reflects that teachers' ICT-integrated competencies start with pedagogy. As teachers apply the latest technologies to enhance the effectiveness and efficiency of teaching, new questions are raised. When and how do teachers adopt and utilise educational possibilities of ICT in their teaching practices and professional development? From a pedagogical perspective, flexible use of technology is likely to facilitate teaching and learning.

Teachers may choose different ways of using technology to achieve various learning objectives under different pedagogical philosophies. Technology use means methods

Table 1: An analytical framework of competency standards

Clustersof Competency	Analytical Framework		
	Major Pedagogy/ Instructional Science	Salient ICT Technology	Major Integration Strategies
Emerging: Integrating productivity tools in learning context	Design authentic & realistic tasks based onpedagogical principles	Demonstrate expertise with ICT productivity tools	Apply productivity tools in learning context
Applying: Enhancing teaching and facilitating learning	Apply learning theory and principles in developing interactive learning environment	Demonstrate expertise with various instructional software development tools	Integrate multimediabased instructional software in different subjects
Infusing: Processing curriculum resources & learning materials	Stimulate learner directed resources for knowledge construction	Demonstrate expertise in developing & organizing web-based flexible learning materials	Integrate open & flexible learning strategies in an online learning
Transforming: Integrating ICT for pedagogical innovations	Incorporate emerging trends in pedagogy and learning principles	Demonstrate expertise with various specialized software	Integrate innovative learning strategies for pedagogical innovation

or techniques to those who favour "teacher-centred" instructive theories; technology use might be more of a philosophy to those who favour "learner-centred" teaching theories, especially constructivism. Different educational viewpoints lead to different approaches and varied learning outcomes. Teachers are not meant for operating as "sages on the stage" in this information age. Taking up roles as mentors, motivators, administrators, and designers of learning means sharing more responsibilities in promoting students' higher learning standards. They are expected to master and continually apply changing technology in the learning environment.

When integrating technology into instruction, there have to be enough learning opportunities for teachers to equip themselves with the necessary skills. It is critical to make teachers realise that incorporating technology into the fabric of classroom activities not only provides opportunities for teachers to enhance their teaching efficiency and effectiveness but also enables them to migrate from the traditional role of directing learning to a new role: facilitating learners to become self-directed. The stages of competency levels reflect teachers' continuous development and assume that from the earliest understanding and experience with ICT, teachers are working in an actual classroom context so that ICT is infused into teaching and learning.

For example, a competency statements is proposed below. It consists of four major competency items under each cluster.

Cluster 1. Integrating productivity tools in learning practices

– Demonstrate expertise in working with productivity tools that are applicable for teaching and learning work.

- Design authentic and realistic tasks-based on pedagogical principles.
- Demonstrate positive attitude in utilising productivity tools for professional competence.
- Demonstrating knowledge and skills of using ICT in ethical, legal and secure ways.

Cluster 2. Enhancing teaching and facilitating learning

- Identify, plan and locate ICT resources to design and manage learner centred instruction and to support diverse needs of learners.
- Demonstrate expertise with various instructional software development tools.
- Design meaningful learning experiences and integrate interactive multimedia learning environments.
- Apply ICT to facilitate a variety of assessment and evaluation strategies.

Cluster 3. Processing curriculum resources & learning materials

- Demonstrate expertise in developing multi-modal resources using ICT to support curriculum.
- Demonstrate expertises in developing web-based open and flexible learning (OFL) materials.
- Stimulate and integrate learner directed research by using ICT to support knowledge construction.
- Use ICT resources to collect, analyse, interpret and communicate findings to improve instructional practices.

Cluster 4. Integrating ICT for pedagogical innovation

- Apply ICT to develop higher order skills and creativity.

- Integrate ICT in meeting the needs of pedagogical innovations and learning strategies.
- Employ specialised software tools to support pedagogical innovation.
- Apply current research on teaching and learning with ICT while planning learning environment.

ICT Infusions

Those responsible for teacher development may work with local teachers to create effective ICT infusions that are *suitable to local context and specific curricula.* Criteria like those given below, refined to the local context and subject area, may be used: (a) to evaluate and improve infusions as they are designed and applied during teacher development, and (b) for the teachers (and their supervisors) to use later as they begin to create infusions with their own students, so that they can evaluate and improve use of ICT within their own classroom context and practice. To evaluate how meaningfully instructional activities are embedded in each discipline, they can be assessed according to the criteria in Table 2 below.

These criteria help teachers think about the value of a learning activity. Activities that generally score well can be refined so that they are even better; those, which are poor, can be revised or abandoned. Again, the rubric can itself be adjusted and refined according to the local context.

Table 2: Criteria for Assessment of Instructional Activities Infusing ICT

1	To what extent is the ICT activity naturally complex and embedded in a real-world context?
2	To what extent do the learners observe and reflect upon their actions?

3 To what extent is ICT contributing to the attainment of specific goals?

4 Do learners engage in this because it is required or because it is of intrinsic interest? 5 Do learners wrestle with new experiences and become more skilled in identifying problems?

6 To what extent do learners spend time engaged with other learners?

7 To what extent do learners improve in their ability to negotiate with other learners? 8 Do learners simply memorise or do they generate hypotheses, evaluate, assess and predict?

9 To what extent is there one 'right' answer, or does the activity foster generation of multiple complex solutions of varying quality that can be analysed and evaluated?

The types of assessment instrument used need to be sufficiently varied and flexible to enable competence to be demonstrated in a variety of ways reflecting the rich diversity of teaching and learning practice. The assessment processes are required to be equitable and affordable so that all potential candidates have the same opportunities in terms of access to assessment. The nature of the assessment process needs to be made clear to all potential assessment candidates in terms of how it operates, what is expected from the candidates and how best to prepare.

A mechanism for detailed feedback to all candidates requires to be established following completion of the assessment. Feedback has to be an integral part of the assessment process and with provision for including opportunities for further development. Involvement of all stakeholders in the assessment process is crucial for assessment of teacher professional standards.

The most critical factor in the successful integration of ICT into teacher education is the extent to which the teacher educators have the knowledge and skills for modelling the use of ICT in their own teaching practices. A well-conceived and sustained programme of professional development is, therefore, required to enable the teacher educators to develop these skills. But since the role of a teacher today is that of a facilitator, it is his/her primary responsibility for integrating ICT in the teaching-learning processes.

The major objectives and guiding principles of professional development is discussed along with the basic strategies and various approaches to capacity building. Professional development can make a powerful difference in performance of both learners and teachers. Capacity building requires sustained and ongoing efforts with support from all the stakeholders of the education system. As such, the perception of teachers to face the challenges of an ICT enriched teaching and learning environment is crucial.

Capacity Building

Teachers constitute the largest professional group in most of the countries of the Asia-Pacific region. Ensuring continuing professional development of teachers presents a formidable challenge by itself. Integration of ICT into the various strategies for teaching and learning not only presents a new set of challenges, but also holds great opportunities that are intrinsic to the nature of the newer ICT. The rapid and inexorable movement towards a knowledge society places new demands on the knowledge, skills and competencies of teachers. At the same time, technology development gives rise to newer opportunities and advantages.

Applications of ICT have served to bridge temporal and spatial barriers that have long mitigated against introduction of new knowledge, approaches and techniques to teachers who work in far-flung areas. Productivity tools can give a teacher more time for professional growth and knowledge enrichment: this is over the time that is now spent on repetitive classroom management tasks. Accessing the global knowledge and information resources requires development of an environment that supports pedagogy-ICT integration at the national, local and institutional levels.

Optimal use of the knowledge tools and resources demands adequate preparation and skills of teachers in order to reap the maximum benefits of the emerging information society. The most important criterion for effective professional development is to tailor it to the learning needs and skill levels of individual teaching staff. This suggests that, ideally, an institution is required to, based on the availability of resources, provide a variety of options for professional development for the teachers. In structuring professional development options and resources, it is helpful to explore collaboration opportunities with partners outside the institution.

The opportunities for ICT to create new paradigms of teaching and learning will depend largely on leadership and a shared vision, and on appropriate and continuing professional development. There are three major components of capacity building objectives:

- The improvement of teachers' knowledge base, their skills and attitudes (KSA) in ICT integration
- The motivation of teachers to apply innovative pedagogical approaches and models in the classroom
- Making teachers competent in developing online/ offline-learning resources. The major objectives of the capacity building are shown in Figure 8.

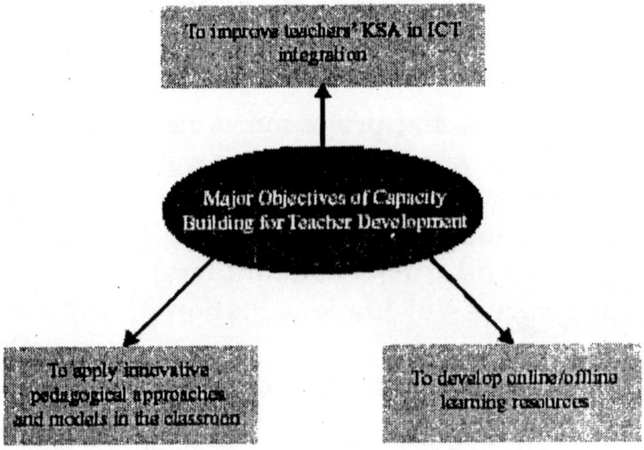

Figure 8: Capacity building for teacher development in ICT integration

Professional Development of Teachers

Professional development refers to a variety of activities, both formal and informal, designed for the personal and professional growth of teachers with respect to pedagogy-technology integration. Professional development includes individual development, continuing education, in-service education or staff development, as well as, various professional developmental activities. It involves a wide variety of curricula to ensure that the teachers acquire and maintain the required competencies to face the diverse challenges of pedagogy-technology integration.

It is concerned with the development of new insights into pedagogy and stimulates an on-going reflection into one's own practices. Various professional development strategies exist for the successful implementation of pedagogy-technology integration. The strategies recognise the diversity within the region in terms of culture, languages and ethnicity. They encourage innovative practices. The strategies also focus on incorporating ICT development, education reforms and professional development of teachers in national policies and plans.

National plans and programmes require taking into account teachers' needs and concerns, particularly those related to their professional development. Commitment and support at various levels (facilitators, policy makers, communities and other stakeholders) are crucial in facilitating successful implementation of any national policy. Teachers may find it impossible to incorporate ICT into their work without support from peers, parents, leaders and other stakeholders. To bring this about, these community members may also need professional development along with the teachers. Countries that have initiated efforts to infuse ICT into teacher education have found the following professional development strategies to be helpful in successful technology integration:

a) Professional development programme on ICT integration places pedagogy over technology. The focus lies in teaching and learning rather than hardware and software alone. In other words, it is not only about mastering ICT skills but also utilising ICT to improve teaching and learning.

b) Professional development of teachers requires adequate access to ICT resources in the classroom. The better the access to ICT, the more likely it will be used for in structional purposes. This is a big challenges across the Asia-Pacific region because of the diversity of institutions and the difference in resources.

c) A 'Just in Time' (JIT) approach to professional development is a model that works well. In this approach, professional development is provided to teachers on a as-and-when-required basis.

d) Capacity building is a sustained, continuing and lifelong process. It is not a one-time activity. Teachers need to update their knowledge and skills as the school curriculum and technology change. Individuals develop in stages and mature over time.

e) Professional development is a building process. Preferably it starts with what teachers do well in the classroom. Teachers can then gradually build their skills and knowledge in successive steps, towards pedagogy-technology integration.

f) Capacity building should be based on learning needs and skills of individuals. A detailed needs assessment is essential in order to identify gaps between the present status and the target to be achieved.

g) ICT has the potential to break the professional isolation from which many teachers suffer. ICT provides a suitable means of connectivity with universities, peers, mentors, centres of excellence and the sources of teaching and learning materials.

While developing professional development strategies, one requires to take into account the following guiding principles to promote pedagogy-ICT integration in its proper context:

- Infuse ICT into the entire teacher education programme: pre-service, in-service, and both formal and informal teacher education.

- Integrate ICT in all activities of education: teaching, learning and administration.

- Empower teachers to develop knowledge, skills and positive attitudes actively towards integrating ICT in teaching and learning.
- Integrate ICT in all aspects of learning, and in all phases of the learning process.
- Integrate ICT for lifelong learning.
- Innovate ICT to embody and model the forms of pedagogy that teachers can use themselves in their classrooms.
- Apply hands-on, learner-centred principles in designing professional development programme.
- Use ICT for empowering teachers to use a variety of learning strategies.
- Apply ICT to promote higher order thinking skills.
- Emphasise the professional development of teachers to reduce the digital divide within and among the member/participating countries.
- Use ICT to remove barriers between learners and facilitators.
- Provide an authentic learning environment for ICT integration.
- Encourage teachers to be mentors, tutors, guides and facilitators.
- Encourage self-directed learning independent of space and time.

Approaches to Capacity Building

There is a variety of approaches to capacity building and an overview of the approaches may prove to be helpful in determining the specific requirements of each country in the context of diverse environments in the region. The various planning guides adopted by the different countries suggest a number of useful approaches for high quality professional development programmes. Some of these are discussed below:

1. Professional development programmes respect and encourage the leadership development of teachers. There is a variety of such roles including mentoring new teachers, acting as consulting teachers, coordinating alliances and networks among teachers, and doing advocacy work etc.

2. A balance between collaborative work and individual learning is required. Central to the professional development enterprise is a learning culture that is collaborative. Examples of collaborative activities are joint planning, problem solving, study groups, team teaching, and participation in alliance.

3. Accountability and evaluation of professional development programmes provide a basis for future planning. All professional development plans have to be evaluated against data about student learning, institutional needs and goals, and teaching and content standard.

Inadequate training is one of the major obstacles to the effective use of ICT in teaching and learning. If teachers do not receive adequate training at the pre-service stage, the learning gaps may be filled through in-service training. The development of ICT influences two important aspects of delivering professional training programmes. One is the way the institutions train prospective teachers and the other is how institutions design continuing education for teachers to learn on-the-job either at the physical workplace or through virtual learning. There are various merits and demerits of different approaches of professional development programmes.

A popular strategy for delivering professional programmes is to provide centralised training offered through direct contact mode. This has limited success unless followed up by training and support for the effective use of ICT by trained teachers. Another useful approach to professional development is school-based training. School-based training is an on-site, customised teacher-training programme for in-service teachers. The training course is arranged in a small group of maximum twenty persons that ranges in duration from 2 to 10 days, depending on the content.

Several organisations such as the Institute for Teacher Education: In-Service Department (UK, Australia), the Princess Sirindhorn IT Project (Thailand), and World Links (funded by the World Bank in various countries) use this approach with their teacher training projects. According to these sources, institution-based training approach is cost-effective. Some factors based on experiences regarding on-site training from Australia, Maldives, Thailand, United Kingdom and the United States are the need for:

- teacher reform policy-putting the emphasis from teacher training organisations to institutions
- teachers' initiative for professional development
- team-work building
- familiarising teachers with computer equipment at the institution

It is difficult for teachers to take time out from their regular teaching schedules to attend extended training courses;

therefore, providing on-site training at their institutions is more convenient and specific to their needs.

Successful models for professional development reflect the holistic nature of capacity building rather than focusing only on technological skills. Mentoring and reciprocal mentoring is an example of a professional development model that builds capacity within an organisation. In the early stages of this process, many teachers develop confidence in working with ICT from the primary level and slowly keep pace with growing confidence and autonomy. ICT has increased the access and flexibility to reach learners any time and anywhere.

Mentorship can be fostered across geographical boundaries by using synchronous and asynchronous interaction. Training programmes can be organised for intensive face-to-face sessions, followed by long term follow-up, using online learning strategies. This hybrid approach to capacity building is becoming popular in most of the developing countries. Apart from the face-to-face, on-site institution-based training, online training and direct mentoring methods, there are various other capacity building exercises. They include:

- exchange programme
- workshop at local, regional, national and international levels
- case study
- web-based learning
- self-directed instructional resources including multimedia packages

While the potential of technology to offer creative opportunities for individual and collaborative learning for teachers is no longer debated, the realities of education in the developing countries in the region include the fact that computers in institutions are inadequate, connectivity is still limited and most other technology resources are unevenly distributed. The following show examples of ways in which teachers can make optimum use of ICT for professional development.

1. Teachers of the same subject area can take turns researching on professional development issues or topics that could be discussed, articles could be downloaded, indexed, hyper-linked to actual sites and saved in staff development folders for using offline.
2. A small number of computers may be set aside exclusively for professional development purposes. Departmental committees may be formed to determine the web-based resources related to ICT integration for professional development purposes.
3. Copies of files and folders of professional development articles and web-based resources can be made available on CDs to rural schools that have no Internet connectivity.
4. Use of an intranet system, which features a discussion or "knowledge forum", can be a useful approach for professional development. Young teachers may seek assistance from experienced teachers by posting questions relating to ICT integration. Teachers can join online study groups where connectivity is strong in order to explore better ways of teaching and sharing experiences.
5. Videos of lessons demonstrating seamless technology infusion in various subject areas can be viewed and critiqued by teachers during staff development meetings.

6. Visits to institutions that have rich pedagogy-technology environments can help to understand and benchmark ICT integration.

An institution can adopt or develop a competency continuum for pedagogy-ICT integration. Based on this, individual professional growth plan of a teacher can be benchmarked. Teacher training institutions, professional societies, institutional administrators and educational policy makers continue to identify, study and disseminate examples of pedagogy-ICT integration that respond to professional needs.

Online Knowledge Resources and Offline Networking

Teachers may find it impossible to incorporate ICT into their work without support from peers, parents, leaders and other stakeholders of the education system. To bring this about, there is a need to form a support group comprising parents, local business groups, NGOs, and the community at large with teachers at the core to facilitate integration of ICT into the teaching and learning system. This will create a local knowledge base for infusing ICT integration. This local knowledge needs to be integrated with regional and international knowledge base of ICT for teacher development.

Regional and international collaboration can provide ongoing mentoring and support for those who lead ICT in teacher education within and outside institutions. They engage in discussions on topics more relevant to their needs and practices such as ways of customising software to local contexts. Such collaborative problem solving among the countries within the region and outside is important to many teachers who have relatively little access to technical support or opportunities to view new developments.

Knowledge can be availed of, extended, shared and transformed using knowledge portals and gateways. Global gateways provide a necessary filter to help reduce information overload. Even more importantly, the filtered information has been evaluated before placement in a portal, and often links to sources and resources are accompanied by brief descriptions. Like the rapid growth in information, the number of web portals has similarly increased and so also guide to online knowledge networks.

The large store of resources at a particular portal is easy to navigate and useful for capacity building. The ICT portal for teachers developed by UNESCO Asia and Pacific Regional Bureau for Education is one example. There is a strong need to develop online teacher resource bases in the area of pedagogy-technology integration at national levels and link them with the portals at regional levels. Content development, teacher designed e-lesson plans, knowledge base on ICT integration and various innovative practices can be shared for effective use of ICT to improve teaching and learning. The best innovative approaches and high quality teaching materials produced by the teachers call for reward and encouragement. Based on experiences, offline networks can be developed in centres of excellence such as universities, research centres and teacher training institutions.

Implications

ICT has provided a new perspective and opportunity to motivate and engage teachers in professional development programmes. ICT can contribute significantly to all the three components of professional development:

– Firstly, it can bring world experiences into professional training by providing good teaching and learning materials, facilitating simulations and capturing and analysing best practices of teaching.

– Secondly, ICT can open a world of flexible lifelong professional development programme by offering training any time and anywhere.

– Finally, ICT can break the professional isolation of teachers by connecting them in a virtual network and with valuable resources of teaching and learning materials.

Unless teachers are given due recognition for the key role that they can play and thus encourage them towards innovation, the transformation level of ICT integration becomes a harder target to reach. In order to create successful programme for capacity building and for teachers to become pioneers, inventors and shapers of the new culture of learning, professional development programmes should consider the following elements:

– inspire teachers to invent.

– focus on experiential learning.

– conduct need assessments.

– provide greater opportunities for feedback and reflections.

– improve teacher competence in ICT integration.

5

ICTs for Mathematics

There has been a considerable history in education of technological 'solutions' being offered to various 'problems' of schools and schooling. Whether with the film strip, the overhead projector or, more recently, with electronic devices of various sorts, technological development is presumed simply placeable in a classroom. It is equally assumed that only good will come of it. The repeated facts of unintended and unforeseen turbulence, of the classroom and the curriculum being an ecology held together, only somewhat stable in a complex and fragile balance are often forgotten when the latest 'saviour' device is introduced.

Portable, batteryoperated calculators have repeatedly been heralded in this guise, first for arithmetic teaching and soon thereafter for much of mathematics. The history of calculators in the UK is not so different from that of microcomputers, not least in terms of the inverse relationship over a relatively short space of time between cost and computational speed and power and the comparable direct relationship between cost and size. The first hand-held, battery-powered, four-function arithmetic calculators appeared in the UK between 1970 and 1972.

The 'scientific' multi-function calculators (which included logarithmic, exponential and various trigonometric functions) became available very soon thereafter around 1972 (with the HP 35 and the HP 65, the latter being both hand-held and programmable). The first graphing (graphical, graphic) calculators emerged in 1985. The following year, Kenneth Ruthven, working at the University of Cambridge, started a school-based research project on 'graphic' calculators, involving this Casio machine. The arithmetic calculator undoubtedly perturbed the traditional number curriculum of the primary school.

During the 1980s, there were a number of projects exploring what children could do when provided with unrestricted access to numerical calculators, as well as examining how the curriculum needed adjusting to their presence. The Calculator Aware Number (CAN) project was the most extensive and successful of these exploratory projects, running from 1986 until 1992. A good example of unforeseen curricular turbulence occurred with regard to 'fractions versus decimals' in the presence of calculators.

Calculators display decimal representations of numbers almost entirely, which markedly privileged this representation when calculators became widespread in classrooms. Consequently, students, who increasingly gained much of their arithmetic experience through interactions with calculators, needed greater emphasis on fraction work elsewhere. Scientific and, subsequently, graphing calculators, which are of far greater relevance to secondary-school mathematics, have only seen somewhat limited usage, due to their relative exclusion from classrooms and examination halls. Currently, the mathematical capability of, say, a TI-92+ calculator far outstrips the expected performance of a successful A-level student. Its wide-ranging functionality also highlights the increasing blurring between the devices of calculator and microcomputer: what actually is the difference when you can run interactive geometry software, link up to the internet, program and much, much more on such hand-held devices?

Use of Computers in Teaching of Mathematics

One widespread experience of the past couple of decades is how changes in technology always seem to outpace pedagogy, not unlike the experience of attempting to walk on a shale hillside. So while a particular teaching/learning approach can emerge either in conjunction with or in response to a particular computer program or application, shifting platforms or operating systems require either continued enhancement or transfer, or the program may simply be lost or left behind. Given this increasingly common pattern, it can, therefore, be interesting to reflect on three particular, partial counter-examples.

During the 1980s, as part of a curriculum development project based in London called Secondary Mathematics Individualised Learning Experiment (SMILE), teachers worked very hard to develop mathematical teaching software for the BBC 'B'/Master or RM 380Z/480Z. These programs were extensively trialled and iteratively modified over time, in response to classroom experience. The common school hardware in the UK evolved first into BBC Archimedes or RM Nimbus machines, then moved to generic PCs, before most recently incorporating hand-held 32K calculators with Flash technology (which allows the downloading of small programs from the internet).

Despite these significant platform changes, the SMILE programs are still widely available and, consequently, the pedagogic thinking that went into them is also still present. This educational thinking has thus been progressively built on rather than simply jettisoned due to the rapidly changing technology. This contrasts with the more recent development of many teaching CD-ROMs, where the pedagogy is relatively underdeveloped.

A second example comes from the work of David Tall, a professional mathematician based at the University of Warwick, who initially single-handedly developed an entirely graphical approach to the calculus, based on visualisation, 'zooming in' on points and the notion of a graph being 'locally straight'. He developed a suite of programs written in BASIC, known as Graphic Calculus, to support his approach. These innovative programs and notions led to a subsequent generation of graph-plotting software which incorporated his ideas, insights and approach.

A third, more extensive example of a pedagogy continuing, deepening and modifying in conjunction with technological development can be seen in the case of the computer language Logo. Nearly 25 years ago, the book Mindstorms: Children, Computers, and Powerful Ideas appeared. In it, Seymour Papert presented a Piagetian-inspired educational philosophy involving children interacting with computers by means of programming in Logo. Students learned mathematics through programming rather than from 'example, exercise and test' methodologies that were incorporated into a traditional computer-aided instruction approach to computer software.

A common starting point in creating Logo programs involved directing and controlling a 'turtle' on the screen. This is an embodiment of what became known as 'turtle geometry', the original Papert Logo microworld. The software provided immediate screen feedback in the light of which students could modify their work. The available language was also extensible: that is, the student's own new procedures could be used as if they were simple system primitives (part of the original tool-kit of commands) within the language itself.

According to Paul Goldenberg, a microworld is 'a well-defined, but limited environment in which interesting things happen and in which there are important ideas to be learned'. Students were set loose to explore interesting, mathematically rich environments. Examples of Logo school microworlds include Newton (modelling turtle motion with forces and masses), 3D-Logo (which adds the primitives pitch, yaw and roll) and LogoGrid (which works with numerical grids and operations upon them). In the UK, books such as Ainley and Goldstein's Making Logo Work provided secondary mathematics teachers with a range of tasks and discussion of related classroom issues, as well as an introduction to the prevailing Logo educational philosophy.

However, a tension remained concerning how overtly mathematical the task of programming the computer was. This concern became especially fraught when subject-matter time was both limited and on the decrease (unlike in primary school, where subject-matter boundaries could be much more fluid). It also became of greater relevance in the UK when, as a consequence of the introduction of the national curriculum for mathematics in 1988, teacher flexibility with regard to content became more significantly constrained. 'Doing maths while learning

Logo' was the title of an article written by Richard Noss and published in Mathematics Teaching, the professional journal of the Association of Teachers of Mathematics (ATM). It captures well some of the early beliefs about school students encountering significant mathematics in the course of learning to write computer programs.

The first core educational arguments emerged between those advocating the mathematical benefits of programming in Logo and those who adhered to the lower-level language BASIC (not so different in its intensity from the subsequent allegiance debates between Mac and PC users). Whether Logo or BASIC, this initial role for computers in the teaching of mathematics became known as 'mathematical programming' and it became common during the 1980s to see claims like 'mathematical programming should be a staple part of mathematics courses in the future'.

The second main tension arose between those who advocated the mathematical benefit of programming computers and those who leaned more towards what were often termed 'short BASIC programs'. These were initially often written either by the individual teacher or by students, in order to illustrate or provide practice in specific mathematical topics. However, the beginning of the separation between program writer and user, echoing the early nineteenth-century musical separation between piano composer and performer, had begun.

Over its 25-year life, Logo has seen various developments, including that of other, related programming media such as Boxer, an attempt to broaden the notion of programming into providing a 'medium of expression'. Boxer attempts to provide a challenging notion of computational literacy, one in which everyone (teachers and students alike) can both create their own educational products, as well as use those created by others.

Sometimes, more recently, dialects of Logo have appeared, for instance to support multiple agents operating in parallel. One such, StarLogo, allows students to control individual 'turtles' on a whole-class display through a wireless graphical calculator network. Another, NetLogo (short for 'Internet Logo') does not require the various 'agents' involved to be physically located in the same room. NetLogo describes itself as 'a programmable modelling environment for simulating natural and social phenomena. It is particularly well-suited for modelling complex systems developing over time'.

Downloadable for free from the internet, NetLogo comes with a sizeable collection of pre-written simulations connected to a wide range of school content. Interestingly, what previously might have been seen as mathematical models or applications can now be seen directly as, say, geography (efficient traffic light flow) or biology (nutrient uptake in sunflowers or honeycombs). One consequence is that the mathematics becomes increasingly hidden within the program itself, apparently falling within the domain of an adult specialist. When the models have been built, they can be saved as internet applets for use in web pages.

One cutting-edge educational possibility is using NetLogo to run a participatory simulation in the classroom, with each student controlling part of the system using a device such as a TI-83+ graphical calculator. Consequently, it is possible now to think of graphical calculators as an interim technology (rather than a free-standing computational device), whose benefits include portability, accessibility and low relative cost.

However, it seems more likely that the graphical calculator will metamorphose into a portable peripheral interface between a person in transit and a more fixed computer. It may also have a growing role as a virtual controller, as with NetLogo. Even back in 1980, there were physical turtles programmable via the computer in Logo.

Various subsequent developments in robotics allow two-way flow of information between the computer and the 'robot', rather than the original turtle which was only able to receive and subsequently act on instructions. Currently, Lego Mindstorms is seen as being in the domain of ICT teachers rather than mathematics teachers. The nature of the required programming (due to the image-based nature of the programming language) is perceived to be less mathematical in nature.

Thus, Logo continues to this day in various guises, but has not had the wide success that had been hoped for in secondary mathematics education. Nevertheless, it is still quite widely used in UK primary schools. Also, although reference to Logo has recently disappeared from the mathematics national curriculum specification, it is still present in the IT national curriculum.

Microcomputers and Mathematics Teachers

At their very outset in the late 1970s, and although this changed fairly quickly, microcomputers initially had no screens and their only output devices were teletype printers. Because no commercial software or applications were available, using computers (or 'computing' as it was often termed) meant programming them. Even before microcomputers appeared, programming was included, for instance, as a topic in the SMP mathematics O-level syllabus in the early 1970s. The syllabus included programming in BASIC. It was often mathematics teachers (whether or not they were also teaching 'computer studies') who were most likely to have the necessary skill and interest to learn how to program them. It was these same mathematics teachers, therefore, who were interested in students encountering the mathematical aspects of the task of programming within the formal school context, rather than seeing it as a topic to be shared and explored among enthusiasts after school, perhaps in a computing club.

Mathematics teachers tended to pick up the computer studies/computer science O-level teaching when the subject first appeared in the mid-1970s. Being a new subject meant that there were no specialist teachers readily available to teach it. The distinction between computers as objects of school interest in their own right (e.g. to physics teachers, to 'computer studies' teachers) and as pedagogic tools for more traditional subject-matter teaching (such as mathematics) is also a long-standing one. Not long after this time, in 1981, one of us was teaching mathematics in a secondary school when the BBC 'B' microcomputer was first introduced to the school.

For the first time in the history of this school, these computers were placed directly in the hands of maths, science and geography teachers rather than the computer studies teacher, because the head specifically wanted them used to enhance the teaching of non-computing subjects. Yet, so close was this initial link between mathematics teachers and computers that, for instance, in 1984, the Computers in the Curriculum project (emanating from Chelsea College in London) deliberately excluded mathematics teachers from consideration, in order to allow other subject-area teachers access to computers to start developing curriculum materials.

Twenty years ago, the authors of an HMI report on mathematics teaching in the sixth form reflected on microcomputers and their potential for reshaping the mathematics curriculum based on what they had seen: The influence that the microcomputer was having upon mathematics [teaching and learning] at the time of the survey was still in the early stages of development.... As microcomputers become more readily available, they will be capable of changing significantly the way mathematics is presented visually in the classroom. Programming procedures will influence the methods used for solving problems and there will be a greater emphasis on numerical techniques. The microcomputer's capacity to store and rapidly reorganise data makes it an invaluable tool to carry out complex statistical and combinatorial investigations. The consequences for mathematics teaching are of the greatest significance and all concerned need to consider carefully how this expensive resource can be used to the best effect.

It is not uncommon for subsequent reality to fail to match up—in whole or in part, in the short or even medium term—to past visionary statements. For example, if the above reference to changed visual presentation of mathematics was intended to signal some sort of 'electronic blackboard' approach, only relatively recently with the broader availability of data projectors and interactive whiteboards has it really become feasible for the whole class to see what is on the computer screen at the same time. Although it is true that availability of computers has somewhat influenced the way mathematics is presented in a classroom setting, the issue of privileging whole-class teaching has led to a difficulty for teachers of mainstream classes.

Whether the situation was one or two computers in a mathematics teacher's classroom or using a computer laboratory facility shared by the school as a whole, it was difficult to work with the whole class, so developments tended to take on an individual flavour. However, politically, there has been a distinction drawn between data projectors running from a lap-top computer and the slightly more recent interactive whiteboard technology, in that there was no government initiative concerned with the former. While acceptable before, in the current era emphasising whole-class teaching, the new availability of interactive whiteboard technology has reinforced this link between political will and technological means.

Because interactive whiteboards are more technically demanding, it may mean computer classroom use will move back to the knowledgeable enthusiast rather than be something for all teachers of mathematics. Alternatively, it may require a reliance on technicians, where available, who have not previously been available to mathematics teachers. In some sense, the data projector is perhaps a more 'democratic' device in terms of its usage requirements. Further, the HMI prediction of greater emphasis on numerical techniques has not manifested itself in the curriculum over the past 20 years. This is primarily due to an unresponsiveness to change in the centralised controllers of the mathematics curriculum, especially at A level which has remained relatively free of numerical techniques.

Many students have voted with their feet, preferring to take statistics or business courses rather than pure mathematics, though even in statistics courses, the potential of ICT use is rarely fully drawn on. A decade after the abovementioned HMI report, the editors of a Mathematical Association report (entitled Computers in the Mathematics Curriculum) once more claimed: 'Mathematics curricula should be able to respond flexibly to technological change'.

Finally, the comment in the HMI quotation about resources is still as significant today as it was then. The most expensive resource is, perhaps surprisingly, not the technology itself. It is the experience of teachers that it can take a good three years for a teacher to train to use technology well -one year to become personally familiar with its features, another year to work with the new device or software in a classroom setting and a third year to reflect on successes and learn from failures.

Over the past 30 years, there have been a couple of shifts in how developments in 'this area' of computer use in relation to teaching and learning mathematics in schools have been referred to and framed. Along with these shifts there have been a number of different ways of justifying school work using computers to teach mathematics. The language of 'computers, computing and computer studies' was first used from the mid-1970s and referred to a separately timetabled school subject with its own syllabus and national examinations.

In 1988, information technology first appeared as the name of a national curriculum subject, and it was also used in 1990 in the context of teaching mathematics in the ATM journal Micromath. However, two years later, in the Mathematical Association document already mentioned, the composite term 'computers/ information technology' was used together with a definition for IT, as if it were a new or unfamiliar term: Information Technology (IT) The storage, manipulation and transmission of data in electronic form. Use includes the use of computer software such as databases, spreadsheets, word-processors, graphic packages but has wider implications in television, radio, telecommunications, satellite transmissions and so on.

IT was still the term used in the School Curriculum and Assessment Authority (SCAA) report on mathematics in the national curriculum and up to 1998 in Micromath 14(1). However, in issue 14(3) later that same year, the term became 'information and communication technology' (ICT). ICT was also used in the government national curriculum document. Oldknow and Taylor comment: Currently the term IT (Information Technology) is being increasingly replaced by the acronym ICT (Information and Communication Technology). In each case it is to emphasise that PCs, and other computers, are just one—albeit very important—element in the range of electronic devices that is revolutionising our society.

Part of the UK's under-documented recent history in this domain involves the question of who taught this emergent and changing subject, as well as what the various foci of the relevant syllabuses were. But equally interesting would be an exploration of the justifications and purposes that were proposed at the time. One question to do with this evolving nomenclature in relation to mathematics is to what extent 'communicating mathematically' is intended to play a part, whether involving direct communication with an electronic device or with other individuals by means of such devices.

The more general issue, concerning which—technology or mathematics—is to be subordinate to the other, was actually addressed in SCAA, which among other things established the various key stages. The authors observed both that 'Pupils should be given opportunities to apply and develop their IT capability in their study of mathematics where appropriate' and that, 'Where appropriate, pupils should be given opportunities to use IT to support and enhance their learning of mathematics'. Thus, we can see a decade ago an official perception of mutual interconnection and subordination one to the other.

One general question which has been around from the beginning is the connection between computers and the world of work and how this impinges on schools. In the 1970s, the work setting involved large mainframes requiring specialist programming and systems analysis. Even as late as 1982, the authors of the Cockcroft report into the teaching and learning of school mathematics were predicting that: Relatively few school leavers are likely to work directly with a computer. Their work will usually be at clerical or operator level dealing with the input and output of data, though some leavers with A-level qualifications obtain posts as junior programmers.... These tasks [related to data handling] demand little in the way of mathematical expertise apart from the need to feel 'at home' with the handling of numerical information. In some cases, it is also necessary to be able to carry out straightforward arithmetical calculations which may involve the use of decimals and percentages.

Successfull Teaching with Technology

Clearly, new teachers are more aware of ICT in general, but there is still a strong need to learn about particular pieces of software or, for example, the use of various data capture/input devices, such as heat probes or other sensors. There used to be a rule of thumb in industry that computer users should only be expected to be familiar with two software packages (to master one, to be familiar with a second). According to Ofsted, by 2002 only one-quarter of schools were putting ICT to good use in teaching mathematics. The authors further claimed that 'only a small proportion of departments has reached the point where they can evaluate critically their use of ICT and decide where it most benefits learning in mathematics'.

However, there has been a steep and rapid increase in home use of ICT. In addition, the needs of industry have been changing rapidly. This has resulted in a tension between student expectations and current mathematics lessons. There is a continuing need for professional development given the pace of change in ICT. The impact of assessment constraints on the uptake of ICT in mathematics in England is still considerable, in contrast with Scotland where ICT is far more integrated into mainstream assessment practices. Assessment of ICT outcomes in England is proving challenging across many subject areas, so it has frequently fallen by default back onto the IT department, where the responsibility for assuring the current 'IT entitlement' customarily resides. But the primary concern for mathematics teachers is related to the need to deploy the technology very carefully.

6

ICTs for Teaching Science

Learning science is about making sense of the world around. Practical work also has a role in learning science through enabling pupils to test, rethink and reconstruct their ideas. Practical work is one way of assisting the crucial process of enabling pupils to explore their own and others' ideas. But it is only one way and there are others such as concept mapping, discussion and debate, using computer programs, writing, role-play, field work and library-based research.

Laboratory work has a role here but only when pupils are consciously involved in designing the work and it has a meaning for them. Only when ideas different from their own are seen by pupils to be more fruitful than their own in explaining phenomena and in making predictions, will they be prepared to adopt them. As has often been pointed out, many scientific ideas are counter-intuitive and on the surface make less sense than pupils' own ideas.

Learning about science is often implicit rather than explicit. It is part of a 'hidden curriculum' of science education, conveyed through the language and methods used in the laboratory. Studies have shown that there is a strong influence of the teacher and of the particular curriculum on children's views about science. Benson found considerable consistency in the views of children within a class and considerable differences between classes. This was ascribed to the choice of activities and class materials made by the teacher which in turn reflect his/her philosophical stance in relation to science.

The influence of classroom materials was demonstrated by Carey et al who showed that 12-year-old children's understanding of how scientific knowledge is constructed was strongly influenced by a teaching unit on the nature of science. However Hodson suggested that there was evidence that teachers changed their approach when teaching classes of different ability, 'Thus, teachers who might adopt a hypothetical-deductive approach with high ability children may adopt an inductivist stance with those they consider to be less able'. If pupils are to learn about science there needs to be more explicit discussion of the models of science which have been embraced in recent history.

The different relationships between theory and experiment in these models are best brought together, according to Hodson, 'by encouraging students to regard theory and experiments as having an inter-dependent and interactive relationship; experiments assist theory-building; theory, in turn, determines the kind of experiments that can and should be carried out'. While providing for pupils to carry out their own investigations can be helpful in achieving this understanding, a number of other activities have an important role. These include historical case-studies, simulations and dramatic reconstructions, materials focusing on the nature of science, discussion of topics where theoretical explanations are controversial and thought experiments.

There is no alternative to pupils undertaking some scientific activity for themselves if doing science is a valued part of science education. Although this will often mean direct manipulation of equipment, relevant experience can be obtained through computer-based activities such as the interrogation of data-bases. Hodson claims that scientists gain a double benefit from engaging in scientific inquiry – an increase in their understanding of scientific activity and in their capacity to do it successfully.

Hodson insists that doing science is a holistic activity: 'in carrying out investigations, scientists refine their approach to the problem, develop greater understanding of it and devise more appropriate and productive ways of proceeding all at the same time'. Therefore it essential for achieving the ability to do science that pupils undertake whole investigations, as individuals or in groups, taking a considerable degree of control of the direction the work takes. Younger and less-experienced pupils need to begin with simple and well-defined investigations, moving to those where they have more control as their confidence grows.

Often science clubs out of normal school time provide this experience successfully, being free from the constraints of class time and formal teacher-pupil relationships. In some cases the choice between demonstration or benchwork by pupils is decided by the type of equipment that is needed. In other cases, where there is a real choice, and either could achieve the purpose of the work, the teacher's style is an important determinant.

Role of Computers

Programs for computer-assisted instruction (CAI) have been

developed since the 1960s to provide individually-paced tutoring in many areas of the curriculum. In traditional CAI, feedback to the student is provided about their answers to questions interspersed in the teaching material. In some programs branches and loops are used to tailor routes through the material in response to the kind of answer given to the questions. More sophisticated programs have the capability of identifying types of error or misunderstanding and of matching further input to them.

In practice, however, there is a limit to the application of these programs beyond, for example, simple arithmetic and other basic skills. Over the years, considerable research effort has been devoted to evaluating the impact of these types of program and metaanalyses of many studies have been carried out by Bangert-Drowns et al and Kulik and Kulik. Their results follow the pattern of other meta-analyses of the effectiveness of CAI in showing a significant effect on achievement in test scores, particularly for students of low-socio-economic status, low-achievers and students with special educational needs.

However, many of the early studies have been criticised for methodological flaws and their relevance to more recent practice, using more powerful, networked computers has been questioned. In relation to science education, recent developments use computers as part of a more varied educational experience rather than as a replacement for classroom and laboratory work. Currently the main applications are word-processing, data-logging, graphing, simulations, modelling, analysing data using databases and spreadsheets and accessing information through the Internet. Some of these have been researched in more depth than others.

Word-processing in Science

Word-processing in science provides all the benefits common to its use in other areas of the curriculum. The particular advantages for science seem to arise when children begin to use word-processing as routine throughout practical work and not just to produce a report at the end.

Data-logging

Research on data-logging leads to several conclusions with implications for the role of practical work in science. The findings of Newton although derived from observations of pupils who were new to data-logging, reflected those of several other studies. Newton observed and tape-recorded the conversations of pupils in the first two years of a secondary school in England. The pupils' investigation involved recording the temperature of gases in two plastic drinks bottles, one containing air and one containing air enriched with carbon dioxide, as they were heated by a 100 watt lamp. They used temperature sensors connected to LogIT data-loggers and computers with appropriate software.

The recordings showed that a large part of the students' talk during data-logging was concerned with how to set up and operate the equipment. Newton suggested that this may have been a result of the novelty of the equipment to the pupils and indeed as a general finding it may be an artefact of the introduction of new technology that will disappear when it becomes a more routine part of pupils' work. The data-logging process has the advantage that pupils see the data being recorded from moment to moment in real time and their attention can be given to the trends and patterns as they appear. This is in contrast with conventional practical work, where the focus of attention is the individual data point.

However, watching lines being created on graphs on the screen can be as unproductive, and indeed boring, as repetitive collecting of readings directly from instruments. Several of the pupils in Newton's study reported not enjoying, 'watching the lines going up or down or staying the same'. The potential advantages of data-logging over conventional practical work are realised only when the teacher mediates the process of making sense of the data as it appears on the screen. The recordings of pupils' talk showed that the pupils' interpretations were more closely related to the experiment when the teacher encouraged them to articulate the meaning of the lines on the graph and to make predictions of the possible effects of changes in the experiment.

One of the obvious advantages of data-logging is that it saves time. Pupils don't have to be watching the screen as data are recorded; indeed this can happen when they are not present. For example, an activity for primary pupils is to record the level of light over a full 24 hours in order to identify the exact time of sunrise and sunset or, for older pupils, the levels of light, temperature and dissolved oxygen in an aquarium. Opportunities to extend primary pupils' experience are particularly rich, given that the use of conventional measuring instruments with sufficient accuracy to be useful in some contexts is not feasible.

Graphing

A direct comparison of three approaches to data collection and graphing was conducted by Barton using samples of pupils from two comprehensive schools in three ability bands aged 12/13 and 14/15. The curriculum area chosen for the study was the measurement of the electrical characteristics of circuit components such as resistors, bulbs and diodes. The three approaches were computer-aided practical work, conventional practical work and a non-practical task giving equivalent information. Comparisons were made in terms of the time spent on different activities and an analysis of the activities using a video-recording of each session. It is interesting that the pupils' reactions towards the non-practical activity were not negative. Barton reported:

> Pupils in both year groups and in all three ability bands enjoyed the activity and were the most outspoken about the drawbacks of practical work. They liked the ability to get more done using the non-practical approach and several commented on the way they tended to get confused and distracted by conventional practical work, particularly one involving wires.

Comparing computer-aided and manual plotting of graphs, Barton found, as might be expected, that manual plotting presented greater difficulty to most pupils, particularly the younger and least able: only the more able older pupils could complete the necessary graph unaided and even then with several errors. The problems presented by graphing meant that pupils were not questioning their data as they recorded it, nor identifying any emerging relationships between the variables being plotted. The attention of the pupils using the computer, by contrast, was not taken by the individual data points but much more by the trends in the data.

There was a further difference between the groups in the matter of realising that in some cases the points would not fit a straight line, which was the first assumption of all the pupils. Those using the computer had the advantage of seeing the graph produced for them and this led them to attempt some interpretation of the different shapes of the lines far more quickly than the non-computer group. Also significant was a time difference, since the manual graphing pupils spent between two and four times longer than those using the computer, the difference being greater for the younger pupils. Barton investigated the effect of the different experience on the ability of three groups to interpret graphs and to use them to make predictions. He summarised his findings as follows:

- For year 10 pupils (14/15-year-olds) of average ability and above, there were no major differences in pupils' ability to interpret graphical data using the different methods.
- Where difference did occur, the extra materials covered by the computer groups resulted in their interpretations containing more detail.
- Handling equipment didn't seem to make any difference to pupils' ability to interpret the graphs.
- Manual plotting tended to emphasise individual data items rather than the continuous nature of the *relationship between the variables.*
- Describing graphs is much more effective where a second graph is present.
- No advantages were observed associated with manual graph plotting.

Simulations

Scaife and Wellington list various types of computer simulation, from direct copies of existing laboratory activities, through simulations of industrial processes, to simulations based on constructs such as ideal gases and frictionless surfaces and ones based on models or theories. They also list the advantages and disadvantages of computer simulations. Advantages relate to costs such as reducing expenditure on consumables and multiple sets of equipment, time, safety, motivation of pupils, control by pupils and management problems. At the same time, the disadvantages relate to the image of reality that the simulations can give. On this point Scaife and Wellington mention in particular:

- Simulations give pupils the impression that variables in physical processes can be easily, equally and independently controlled.
- Users can only manipulate the factors and variables that are built into the model; they cannot tamper with the model itself.
- Any model is an idealisation of reality and ignores certain features in order to concentrate on others. This can be misleading and represent a caricature of reality rather than a representation of it.
- Pupils are almost certain to confound the programmer's reality with reality itself.
- These dangers are even greater when the simulation is of a model which is itself an idealisation of reality.

The simulation of an everyday phenomenon was used in an investigation by Lewis et al. They developed what they described as 'a computer-based curriculum' to encourage students' deeper learning of thermodynamics. Their hypothesis was that:

> an opportunity to actively investigate naturally occurring problems using computer simulations, combined with

> activities that encouraged students to directly consider their prior experiences, would encourage students to construct a more robust view of thermodynamics.

Their reformulated curriculum on thermodynamics had three main components: practical datacollection integrated with computer simulation of the same everyday phenomena; using the computer simulation for prediction and reflection and a computer notebook to record the prediction and results; and a model for heat flow introduced, not by computer, but during classroom discussions. The students worked in fours and within the groups each member was assigned an individual role at any one time. Five classes used the computer-based program for a semester and their performance on tests was compared to that of a similar group who studied the regular curriculum on thermodynamics in the previous semester.

The results showed that the students using the computer had increased their performance over previous students in explaining naturally occurring phenomena and in drawing cooling curves. Their performance in explaining heat and temperature graphs correctly was similar to that of the previous students, which was taken as a positive outcome since the computerbased work had given less coverage to relevant variables. Evidence of several kinds supported the view that there was 'an increase in students' integrated understanding'.

Probable reasons for this proposed by the authors were: the greater number of simulated experiments that students could carry out on the computer compared with real-life experiments; the inclusion of real-world simulated phenomena; the concrete nature of the experiments; and the laboratory notebook which facilitated the re-use of ideas. However the researchers' expectations were not met in several other respects:

- students often did not understand that they should be reflecting upon what they found
- the students had difficulty knowing what they should be giving attention to
- they were not very good at testing their own hypotheses and 'debugging their own knowledge'
- they often extended the interpretation of their results so as to confirm their own ideas
- there was little evidence of the students' use of the model of heat flow that was offered.

Modelling

Modelling differs in intent from simulation, although in some cases the distinction is blurred. In modelling, pupils are able to work out for themselves how variables relate to each other, whereas in simulations they are looking at the outcomes of manipulating the model built into the program. Ogborn has given a general discussion of the role of modelling in science education. Scaife and Wellington discuss the role of the computer in modelling, which they suggest should be to take on the 'inauthentic labour' of programming, calculating and presentation, leaving 'the user to focus on the intellectually creative task of devising and exploring the model'. The Model-based Analysis and Reasoning in Science (MARS) project, reported by Raghavan and Glaser is considered here since it makes use of interactive computer activities as a central part of the curriculum units that it has developed.

However, the major thrust of the project is to develop conceptual understanding and model-based reasoning starting from students' existing ideas and so it could equally be placed in the section on constructivism. The argument in favour of enabling students to recognise and use theoretical and explanatory models in science is based on the role that these play in the work of scientists and on the advocacy of science educators:

> Scientists and researchers in many disciplines frequently rely on modelling and model-based reasoning to concretise abstract ideas, to simplify and clarify complex phenomena, to predict trends, and to explain mechanisms and processes... Furthermore, national projects working to reform science education recommend that science educators become less concerned with the presentation of a wide variety of facts and more concerned with overarching themes, and strongly advocate the development of an appreciation for the centrality of models in the teaching and learning of science.

The use of computer programs means that all students can be provided with similar experiences, which is otherwise less feasible, although theoretically possible. The MARS curriculum material provides a 'script' for students, who work through the activities in pairs. Each topic is introduced through practical activities designed to elicit the students' existing ideas about the concept involved. These are followed by computer-based activities and assignments which introduce the scientific view and give the opportunity for students to grasp and 'play with' the model on the screen.

For example, the unit on 'net force' first introduces the idea of using arrows to indicate the direction of a force and a label on the arrow to indicate its strength. Then the computer shows a combination of pushes and/or pulls acting on a ball and the students are challenged to replace the combination by only one force that has the same effect on the ball. They can alter direction and strength of the force and then run their model to see its effect, doing this as often as they wish. After the computer activity they return to practical activity or to a concrete application of the concept. By working through units of this kinds, it is claimed that:

> ...students not only learn to deploy models to analyse, predict, and explain phenomena but also recognise the need to modify or extend a model or a system of models and the inherent rules to account for new and increasingly complex situations.

The teacher's role in these activities is described as being to move around the classroom answering questions, providing help where needed, providing 'appropriate scaffolding', monitoring students' progress, and getting insights into particular difficulties. The curriculum units were trialled and implemented in five grade 6 (aged 11/12) classes and data about the conceptual learning, model-based reasoning and transferability were collected. There was no *control group in the study.*

Preliminary findings indicated that there was an improvement in the students' levels of model understanding, using the levels identified by Grosslight et al. However many of the students only used models after being prompted, while some did this spontaneously. Not surprisingly, this was taken as an indication that in order to promote more spontaneous use of models as reasoning tools, appropriate activities should be embedded in science activities more widely. It was also found that more class time was required for the computer-based units than for the same material taught in the regular way. However teachers had more time to circulate and observe students at work, point out inconsistencies, challenge false assumptions and encourage student reflection.

No doubt the computer had an important role in the MARS project because of the facility it provided for making abstract models available for students to manipulate. However this study also pointed to important aspects of any learning experiences which aim at the development of understanding in pupils—the opportunity for students to work out and test out their own ideas and compare them with the scientific view and the role of the teacher in promoting their engagement with ideas and phenomena and reflective thinking. A project with a similar aim, the Conceptual Change in Science Project, took place in the UK from 1988 to 1991.

A combination of computer-based activities and actual practical work was created and implemented in this collaborative project, involving researchers from the University of Glasgow, The Open University and the University of Leeds. The set of activities, designed to teach mechanics to 12 and 13-year-olds, included both a simulation package and computer modelling software. The curriculum materials comprised worksheets for both the computer activities and the conventional laboratory experiments. The simulation program content was determined after extensive study of pupils' prior conceptions of forces and motion. Four 'scenarios' were then designed to address particular preconceptions.

Laboratory experiments were designed based on the scenarios, requiring pupils to make predictions, give reasons for their predictions and then check the outcome. After development trials, the materials were implemented for seven weeks with a class of twenty-nine 12-year-olds, spending five hours of class time per week on the materials and using five computers. The class was organised so that pupils worked in threes, spending half their time on practical work and half on the computer program. For comparison there were three control groups who were also studying mechanics, although there was no attempt to match either the pupils or the type and duration of activities.

All pupils were given a pre-test, an immediate post-test and a delayed post-test. They were also interviewed about their ideas. The findings showed 'a significant amount of conceptual change' in the experimental class in the form of a significant increase in the number of correct responses and explanations based on Newtonian theories in both the post-test and delayed post-test. Also the pupils' confidence in their answers increased. There was a decrease in two prior conceptions—the claim that motion implies force, and the neglect of friction as a force opposing motion. However, some new incorrect conceptions appeared.

Of the control classes there was one which showed a significant increase in the number of correct responses in the post-test, but no decline in any of the prior misconceptions. The researchers noted that their results, 'came mostly from the examination of the test data. The analysis of the transcribed interviews provided clear confirmatory evidence in support of this, suggesting that the written test data provide an accurate picture of the pupils' understanding'. Their conclusions include the positive one that, 'it is possible to use simulated computer experiments to augment usefully conventional classroom experiments'. At the same time, there was the depressing finding that the nature of the pupils' conceptions relating to force and motion were very different from the higher levels of understanding assumed in secondary science curricula. The implication for practice is that far greater study time is needed if there is to be the required conceptual change.

Spreadsheets and Databases

Spreadsheets can assist in modelling, enabling pupils to

change parts of the model step by step. Goodfellow has described spreadsheets as occupying the middle-ground between simulations and modelling. They also have other functions similar to databases in the manipulation of data that they facilitate. Carson discusses such uses suitable for age groups 11 to post-16, while Swain describes the use of a spreadsheet for the simulation of a complex chemical reaction in an activity suitable for post-16 students.

Authors and users of databases and spreadsheet programs claim considerable benefits from their use by pupils, particularly in facilitating independent working and collaborative working in groups. However, although some research has involved the use of spreadsheets and databases in connection with other computer programs, it appears that there is little research specifically on the effect of these particular types of program.

Internet

The use of the Internet is probably the fastest growing area of IT application in schools, as elsewhere. A useful outline of practices, up to 1997, is provided by Jackson and Bazley. It is perhaps premature to look for research into the impact of these new practices on pupils' learning, but it is difficult to imagine that the increased opportunities provided to both pupils and teachers for access to information, for communication and for collaboration will not have a positive effect on teaching and learning. Some of this is evident in the effort being made by schools to make access easy and 'safe' for pupils, as through the downloading of information selectively from the Internet into a school-wide intranet.

School On-Line is a source of information for both teachers and pupils, offering a question-and-answer area, on-line projects and a useful library of links to various sites. In Scotland, the Science On-Line Support Network (SOLSN) was developed specifically to help primary teachers. It provides an online library of selected materials and links to other websites, an email facility which can be used by teachers to ask questions of 'helpers' who have volunteered to respond, opportunities to read others teachers' questions and the responses to them, a notice-board, and the opportunity to exhibit classroom materials and view materials provided by other schools.

Developments of this type are multiplying daily but it is too soon to have research evidence of the detail of their impact on science education. An evaluation of the feasibility trials of SOLSN indicated that, despite technical problems which prevented schools from taking full advantage of the SOLSN, teachers were optimistic about the effects on classroom practice. Teachers needed help not only in using the software, but in framing questions to ask and deciding what was suitable materials for posting on the website. Further, the primary teachers felt the need for continued personal contact by phone or visits and so it was suggested that local school clusters provide natural groups of schools to take advantage of the SOLSN facilities, with secondary schools taking an active role in providing information, loaning equipment and working together with its primary schools to improve the quality of science teaching and particularly primary-secondary continuity.

Multimedia

Hartley, in a review of the use of multimedia in science education, quotes the definition of Latchem et al that interactive multimedia means: a range of video-disk, compact-disk and computer based systems that allow the creation, integration and manipulation of text, graphics, still and moving images, sound and feedback clues for many diverse applications in education and training, public information and archiving, and point-of-sale and marketing.

Such a wide selection of stimuli, with the computer combining them in a way that gives the user some control over them, clearly has enormous potential in science education. Not only can there be simulations, but pictures of real places, events and processes, with authentic sound. The importance of pictures has been demonstrated in research by Standing et al who found that a five-second exposure to each of a series of pictures, followed by a recall test, produced more than 90% correct recall even when the number of pictures exceeded 2,500. This visual assistance to memory is used in techniques for remembering which rely on linking words to a visual image.

However Bottrill and Lock found that pictures without sufficient supporting context did not allow the students to make effective use of the visuals; there needs to be a link to both the visual and meaning in words. Blisset and Atkins examined the use of video-disc designed to aid understanding of probability and found that 51% of the time was spent 'reading, watching and listening' to the videodisc. Discussion time was largely devoted to what to do to use the video-disc rather than to discussion of the ideas being presented. Similar findings arose from the Conceptual Change in Science Project which developed software to improve students' understanding of motion.

Students' discussions were about, for example, how to change graphical displays, and did not necessarily impinge on the students' conceptions. The researchers concluded that the effective use of multimedia in the classroom requires 'the intellectual academic roles of the teacher to remain as important as ever.' These findings are supported by those from research into interactive multimedia in the very different context of a history lesson on World War 2.

In order to secure the active participation of the student that is necessary to increase learning, multimedia packages may require students to make notes, search for keywords, answer questions, give explanations or solve problems. These requests can made via offline worksheets but they can also be made on-line so that the whole package of exercises and teaching material provides what is described as an 'electronic workbook'.

Constructivism

Constructivist ideas about learning have such a hold on current views that cognitive development is commonly equated with constructivism in action. Constructivism embraces a very wide range of aspects of teaching.

More than two decades of research into children's understanding in science have had a considerable impact on views of learning. The first substantial wave of work in this area since Piaget has been well reviewed by Driver and Easley, Driver and Erikson and Gilbert and Watts. The outcome of this work which is most relevant in the current context is not the details of children's ideas about particular topics, but the consistency in findings of studies from across the world. This has led to universal recognition that pupils are not without ideas about the events and phenomena in the world around them. They do not arrive in the classroom or laboratory with vacant slots in their minds into which new ideas can be poured by teachers, or created by 'discovery' from personal observations. Rather they have their own ideas, but often these are what may be called 'everyday' ideas. Children have formed these ideas in making sense of their everyday experiences because these ideas generally 'work' and are adequate in the context of everyday life. These everyday ideas are often different from scientific theories and there is much evidence that they interfere in learning science.

In Piagetian terms, what often happens is that pupils assimilate new experiences into their present ways of thinking rather than accommodating to new experience by a modification of ideas. Consequently the attention of science educators has turned to how to bring about change or development in ideas, that is, to ensure that children modify their view to accommodate new experience. Piaget suggested that it was necessary to create disequilibrium in order to bring about development of ideas. Those who prefer not to use Piagetian terms, on account of disagreement with other aspects of Piaget's theories, speak of the need to create 'dissonance'.

Much research has focused on the various ways of bringing about dissonance in just the right amount, so as to avoid too great a conflict with pupils' ideas or too little challenge, both of which lead to no learning taking place. However, at the same time, research into the nature of pupils' own ideas and reasoning has continued and it is relevant to summarise what is now known about them before proceeding to approaches to change. There is some consensus from research studies that the characteristics of children's everyday ideas and ways of thinking which have implications for learning science are as follows:

- Several research studies have established that these ideas are 'domain-specific'. Children use different ways of explaining events in different situations although these events are scientifically explained by the same idea. For example, young children use different ways of explaining the 'disappearance' of water from clothes on a clothes line, from a puddle on a path or from an uncovered fish tank.

- Children's ideas are influenced by direct everyday experience.
- Children are not aware of their ideas as ideas: 'they do not appear to know that their explanations of physical phenomena are hypotheses that can be subjected to experimentation and falsification. Their explanations remain implicit and tacit'. This leads to the argument that development of awareness by pupils of their own thinking is important in cognitive development.
- Initial and 'everyday' ideas are not always replaced when conflicting evidence is available; new ideas may be added while children hold on to earlier ideas.
- Reasoning is linear, with explanations being given in terms of a cause bringing about an effect in a sequence of time. 'Students explain, for example, that when the plunger of a syringe is pulled out this creates a vacuum. The vacuum then draws liquid into the syringe'. This type of sequential cause-effect reasoning is quite different from that assumed in scientific explanations which are based on relationships often expressed as a model or theory.

Turning to the approaches to creating 'dissonance', Strike and Posner list four major conditions for bringing about change in ideas:

- there must be dissatisfaction with existing conceptions
- a new conception must be minimally understood, a person must be able to see how experience can be restructured by a new conception

- a new conception must appear initially plausible, to have the capacity to solve problems that provoked dissatisfaction in the old one
- a new conception should suggest the possibility of being fruitful, of opening up new areas of thinking and explanation.

In order for the teacher to know what is likely to meet these conditions it is necessary to find out what the pupils' existing ideas and experiences are. Various teaching sequences have been proposed all of which begin with some 'scene setting' and proceed to encouraging pupils to describe and explain what they know and think about the subject in hand. The sequence produced by the Children's Learning in Science Project is reproduced in Figure 1. Those parts of this sequence which are concerned with inputting a different view and persuading pupils to accept it remain open to different interpretations.

Previously various strategies have been proposed by other researchers for changing pupils' ideas once they have been revealed. An early strategy was to introduce an event or phenomenon which conflicts with the pupils' view in the expectation that the discrepancy would be enough to cause a modification in thinking. It is probably the case that few would regard this as sufficient even if there is only a small gap between the pupils' ideas and those required for scientific understanding. Other ways of using the discrepant event more actively have been suggested, such as following it by group discussions, brainstorming and then debating ideas, charting ideas coming from the class and 'interpretative discussion'.

Hodson provides a summary of a sequence of teaching moves designed to bring about conceptual development and modification in students' through exploring the extent to which their existing ideas are a basis for explanation and prediction. Three cautionary notes about discrepant events are worth adding. Fensham and Kass point out that what may seem discrepant to the teacher may not be so to the pupil.

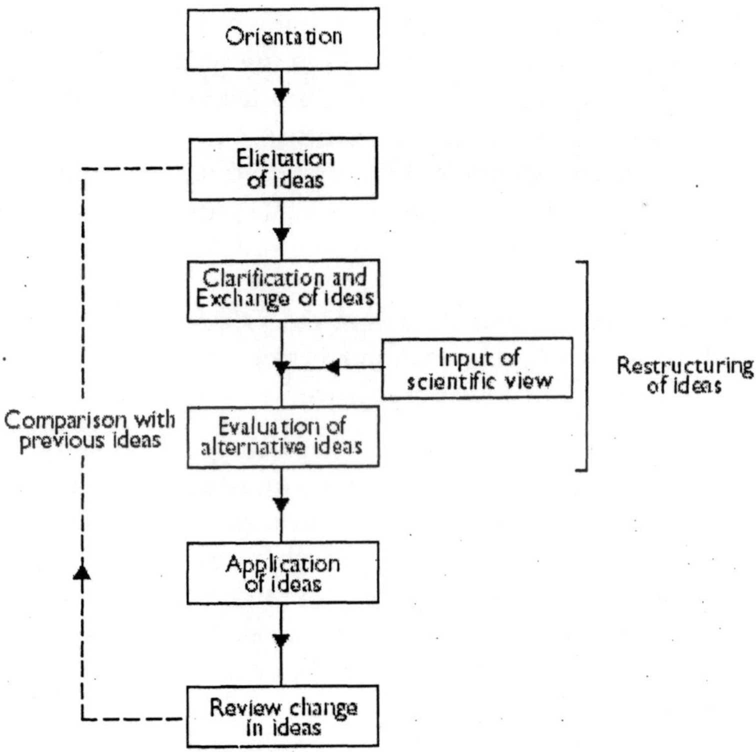

Figure 1: The Children's Learning in Science Project constructivist teaching sequence

Moreover, pupils are more tolerant of exceptions to their views than are scientists and so may not see a need to change their ideas simply because an exception has been demonstrated. Solomon and Simpson raise an objection on more ideological grounds, that the notion of conflict between ideas and the subsequent decision as to which one 'wins' is unsound as a basis for learning. Certainly it would not seem to aid pupils' ownership of ideas.

Watts and Bentley caution against too direct an assault on pupils' ideas. They emphasise that a non-threatening learning environment is important for learning and that dissatisfaction with existing conceptions is not sufficient motivation for change in ideas. Quoting Strike and Posner they point out that alternative ideas must not only be seen as 'plausible, intelligible and fruitful', but the process of adopting them involves 'temporary advances, frequent retreats and periods of indecision'. Thus pupils need a good deal of reassurance and a supportive atmosphere if they are to expose their own ideas and publicly change them. These cautions have particular force at the primary level where much of what pupils encounter is new to them and it is important to build their confidence in being able to make sense of their experiences.

Finding out what children's ideas are in order to 'confront' them is not the same as requiring children to use and test their ideas, as a result of which the ideas may be modified or perhaps abandoned in favour of ones which they decide better fit the evidence available. The Science Processes and Concepts Exploration (SPACE) project researched primary pupils' ideas and, working with teachers, developed techniques for helping children to modify their ideas. One of the areas of uncertainty in constructivism has been the role of the teacher.

To date, however, there is no research to show that one approach to changing pupils' ideas is more effective than another nor that any has long-term effects on the development of concepts. Research in the interdisciplinary field of cognitive science, for example, has in recent years provided convincing evidence that the human processing of visual, linguistic and other data entails the active fitting of such input into a rich internal framework of 'real world' knowledge and expectations, and not simply passive assembly of a mass of external data into an emergent whole. Our understanding of human learning has similarly evolved from a process based on the passive assimilation of isolated facts to one in which the learner actively formulates and tests hypotheses about the world, adapting, elaborating and refining internal models that are often highly procedural in nature.

Acceleration of Cognitive Development

This approach to improving achievement in science is associated in the UK with the work of Philip Adey and Michael Shayer. Their work in the Cognitive Acceleration through Science Education (CASE) Project is of a quite different order from previous attempts to accelerate cognitive development in that it involved intervention over an extended period of two years and explored short-medium and longer-term effects and transfer of effects to other subjects across the curriculum.

The work on cognitive acceleration developed out of their work on Piagetian levels of cognitive development. They considered that, from the growing knowledge of the course of cognitive development and what affects it, there should be the possibility of finding ways of training which accelerate it. Shayer was particularly influenced by Feuerstein's Instrumental Enrichment Programme. Large differences between experimental and control groups on a test of Piagetian tasks had been obtained using this programme, although no effects on school achievement had been found.

However there was enough evidence to suggest that 'the possibility of teaching general thinking skills was worth pursuing, and that what have recently come to be referred to as Higher Order Thinking Skills are well characterised by Inhelder and Piaget's descriptions of formal operations'. In order to give their idea a practical test they designed a set of intervention activities intended to develop higher levels of thinking. For various reasons, including their own background subject expertise, Adey and Shayer set these activities in a scientific context although they were of the view that the skills were general ones which would help thinking across the curriculum.

Student Assessment

Assessment of students has a number of different purposes which can be spread along a dimension from directly helping teaching and learning to summarising and certificating achievement at a particular time. Some summative assessment is used for evaluative or accountability purposes. The concern in the present context is with assessment which affects teaching and learning and, while it can be argued that certification and accountability have an influence on these, the main direct influence is from formative assessment and so the discussion here will be restricted to this.

The definition used by Black and Wiliam identifies the key components of formative assessment: ...the term 'assessment' refers to all those activities undertaken by teachers, and by their students in assessing themselves, which provide information to be used as feedback to modify the teaching and learning activities in which they are engaged. Such assessment becomes 'formative assessment' when the evidence is actually used to adapt the teaching work to meet the needs. Formative assessment in this sense is clearly central to constructivist teaching since this involves finding out pupils' initial ideas and skills. Similarly it is implied in all child-centred work following the Plowden principle to 'begin where the child is'.

However Paul Black questioned Harry Black's claim that formative assessment has always been part of the practice of teachers. Indeed Harry Black himself reported a survey of assessment policies in Scotland which showed that only 29% of schools had a policy on non-reported assessment whilst 87% had one for reported assessment. An even smaller percentage (about 8%) included non-reported assessment in a written policy. The practice of formative assessment is very varied. It often takes the form of short teacher-made tests and although there is evidence that feedback from such tests can improve learning the validity of such tests is often suspect.

They frequently do not reflect the complexity of ideas or skills that the teaching is intended to develop. However Black cites various studies which show that written questions do improve students' learning in a variety of contexts: ... in traditional lessons, with computer animated lessons, with self-study of texts and in learning from chart representations. Questions seem to help by promoting selective attention, by cueing retrieval and by guiding mental editing of new knowledge. A meta-analysis of 40 studies by Bangert-Drowns et al showed performance on external tests does improve with enhanced use of classroom testing. The findings of these studies have to be treated with caution as long as the details are unknown and the possibility remains that the classroom testing was in effect drilling for the external tests.

While traditional written questions may continue to have a role, it has been recognised in the US particularly that new methods of teaching in science require a change in methods of assessment. In the UK, a programme which combined assessment and the development of process skills at the primary school level was given extensive trials and led to the publication of books for teachers on written and practical tasks. Other materials have been produced to help teachers with new methods of assessment, matching new approaches to teaching. However, as Black points out, such materials are in need of rigorous evaluation. He suggests it is necessary to determine whether they can satisfy important conditions: of classroom feasibility, reliability, validity, absence of bias, attention to motivational and affective as well as cognitive development and ways to develop pupil self-assessment.

Black and Wiliam reviewed evidence relating to current practice, drawing on the reviews by Black and Crooks. They listed the following shortcomings of existing approaches, which are quoted in full since not only do they resonate with experience but they suggest ways in which practice can be improved:

- Teachers' tests encourage rote and superficial learning: this is seen even where teachers say they want to develop understanding—and many seem unaware of the inconsistency.
- The questions and other methods used are not discussed with or shared between teachers in the same school and are not critically reviewed in relation to what they actually test.

- For primary teachers particularly, there is a tendency to emphasise quantity and presentation of work and to neglect its quality in relation to learning.
- The giving of marks and the grading functions are overemphasised, while the giving of useful advice and the learning function are under-emphasised.
- Approaches are commonly used in which pupils are compared with one another, the prime purpose of which appears to them to be competition rather than personal improvement.
- Teachers' feedback to pupils often seems to serve social and managerial functions, at the expense of the learning functions.
- Teachers are often able to predict pupils' results on external tests—because their own tests imitate them—but at the same time they know too little about their pupils' learning needs.
- The collection of marks to fill up records is given greater priority than the analysis of pupils' work to discern learning needs; furthermore, some teachers pay no attention to the assessment records of previous teachers of their pupils.

However, despite the shortcomings of existing practice, Black and Wiliam did find strong evidence that '...formative assessment is an essential feature of classroom work and the development of it can raise standards'. In their review, Black and Wiliam helpfully reported evidence for this claim and also identified significant features of the operation of formative assessment that appear to make it effective in improving learning. The evidence from at least 20 studies is remarkably consistent in pointing to substantial and significant gains from innovations which include strengthening the practice of formative assessment.

Black and Wiliam calculate that the size of the effect on performance is larger than for most other educational interventions—for example, it would raise the position of a pupil from among the average to being in the top 35%. Some studies involved children with mild learning difficulties and these children benefited particularly from the improved formative assessment. The possibility of reducing the spread of attainment is a feature which deserves serious attention, given the greater spread of achievement in Scotland compared with other countries.

Black and Wiliam concluded from the evidence they reviewed that: it seems clear that very significant gains could lie within our grasp. The fact that such gains have been achieved by a variety of methods which have, as a common feature, enhanced formative assessment, indicates that it is this feature which accounts, at least in part, for the successes. At the same time these researchers pointed out the considerable difficulties of widespread adoption and take-up of formative assessment since several features of effective formative assessment require quite fundamental shifts in teachers' views of how children learn and, particularly, the benefits of giving the pupils a role in their own assessment.

On this point Black makes the cogent comment that: Teachers need the confidence that they can make anyone learn as long as they go about it the right way, confidence that is needed because devotion to formative assessment is risky, taking a great deal of time and energy. In particular, since many pupils may have acquired the habit of doing just enough to get by, or have ceased to believe that they can be competent at the subject, the contract between teacher and pupil has to be reformulated.

On the basis of their review Black and Wiliam make suggestions as to how formative assessment can be improved. These are discussed under three headings: the self-esteem of pupils; self-assessment by pupils; and the evolution of effective teaching. In relation to self-esteem, the main point arises from the form in which assessment is reported to the pupils. Where this is in terms of grades or ranking within the class then 'pupils look for the ways to obtain the best marks rather than at the needs of their learning which these marks ought to reflect'. Research has given many examples of how pupils spend time looking for clues to the 'right' answer and for the easiest ways to obtain credit.

Moreover those who get poor results feel that this is a judgement of their ability and they can do nothing about it. These negative effects can be avoided by giving feedback only about the particular aspects of the work, with discussion on how it can be improved and making no judgemental comment on the child as a person or in comparison with others. Self-assessment is still at an early stage of development but Black and Wiliam regard it as an essential part of formative assessment. Sadler is quoted by Black and Wiliam helping understanding of the role of self-assessment in learning by identifying three necessary elements of feedback on learning: knowing what the desired goal is, knowing where one is in relation to this goal and knowing how to close the gap.

The extent of good practice in implementing these forms of feedback is limited, but Black and Wiliam claim that: When pupils do acquire such overview, they then become more committed and more effective as learners: their own assessments become an object of discussion with their teachers and with one another, and this promotes even further that reflection on one's own ideas that is essential to good learning.

In relation to improving practice, the outcomes of their review lead Black and Wiliam to emphasise planning which includes formative assessment. 'Tasks have to be justified in terms of the learning aims that they serve, and they can only work well if opportunities for pupils to communicate their evolving understanding are built into the planning'. There are also implications for teachers' questioning and the kind of dialogue between teacher and pupils, which 'should be thoughtful, reflective, focused to evoke and explore understanding, and conducted so that all pupils have an opportunity to think and to express their ideas'.

In addition, classroom tests and homework exercises should reflect the learning aims and feedback on them should be given to pupils following the principles already mentioned. Research has clearly shown that feedback in the form of comments only, leads to higher achievement as compared with feedback in terms of grades or praise or no feedback at all.

Feature of Effective Teaching

Planning, questioning and the use of language are the main features of effective teaching.

Planning

Planning, and support for planning, emerge as features of primary science practice in need of improvement and where action might well pay dividends. Current planning focuses on what children will do and not on what they will learn nor on how the teacher will facilitate children's learning. Better planning would include:

- what ideas the activity would help to develop
- what skills the activity would help to develop
- how the children's initial ideas would be elicited
- what questions the teacher would ask, when and for what purpose
- what classroom organisations are appropriate at different points of the lesson
- what equipment is needed
- what and how instructions would be given to the children
- how the children will record and report their activities
- how the plenary discussions will be handled
- how any change in children's ideas and skills will be monitored.

While planning this amount of detail may seem a tall order for many teachers it is difficult to see how effective teaching can proceed without at least the factors listed above being thought through beforehand. The initial steps require teachers themselves to understand the concepts involved in the pupils activities. If they don't have this knowledge it is available in books specifically written for primary teachers. Using these and other sources, as the need arises, could gradually improve background understanding without teachers feeling the need to learn about all areas of science before they can begin.

Teachers' Questions

The quality of teacher's questions has been the subject of several studies. Moreover the pattern of teachers' question-

and-answer itself controls student behaviour and enforces rules of interaction that makes science learning into a kind of game in which learners attempt to guess the ideas that she is thinking. Thus teaching that is concerned with learners developing their understanding has to avoid closed, low-level questions which take away the learners' control for developing their own ideas.

Types of questions which help rather than hinder this development are, in form, open and person-centred and, in content, require reasoning skills, prediction, interpretation and argument. The quality of teachers' questions has been related to teachers' knowledge of the subject-matter. Teachers with high content knowledge ask fewer questions and encourage more questions. Low levels of teacher understanding of the subject matter were related to asking low-level questions designed to serve the purposes of classroom management. Teachers are more likely to use whole class teaching for topics where they have greater knowledge of the subject matter.

Pupils' Questions

The importance of encouraging pupils to ask questions has been pointed out by several science educators. Through the study of pupils' questions Watts et al identified three categories which can be used for this diagnosis. These are, first, consolidation, where pupils are moving toward consolidation of their ideas on a particular subject. Questions of this kind express what pupils think and ask for confirmation of their explanations. The second type are questions for exploration where ideas are quite firmly held and are used to make predictions which the pupils are seeking to test in the questions asked. The third type, elaboration, are asked when pupils are making up their minds about certain ideas and are examining pros and cons.

These authors recognised that encouraging pupils to ask questions may be disruptive to lesson plans and so propose strategies for dealing with such interruptions without discouraging questioning. These include a specific time for free questioning within a lesson, a 'question box' in the classroom, pupils asking questions of each other in a turn-taking structure and 'question-making' homework. Although Watts et al did not investigate any effect of question raising on student achievement, there have been several studies in the US of such effects.

Role of Spoken Language

The work of Barnes in drawing attention to the importance of talking to develop learning has lost none of its relevance. He was concerned with language in all settings, both in discussion among pupils and between pupils and teacher. By studying children's speech when involved in group tasks, Barnes showed how individuals contribute to the shared understanding of an event or process. One pupil's idea may be taken up by another and elaborated; it may perhaps be challenged by someone else and lead to the group seeking evidence to see which idea stands up to being tested.

With several minds at work there is less chance of ideas being tested in a superficial manner than if a pupil is working alone with no-one to challenge how things are done. The challenge can only be made if the thinking is public, that is, through talk which is under the control of the pupils. Encouraging genuine collaborative group activity is important to achieving the kind of interchange which develops ideas. Barnes also pointed out that working in groups, of itself, will not serve this purpose. There has to be a structure which facilitates learners' reflection on what they have done and requires experience of 'representing' it to themselves.

He added: There seems every reason for group practical work...normally to be followed by discussion of the implications of what has been done and observed, since without this what had been half understood may soon slip away. Talk and writing provide means by which children are able to reflect upon the bases upon which they are interpreting reality, and thereby change them. Henderson has suggested several strategies for promoting group collaboration and class discussion, including:

- groups researching a topic and presenting their findings to the rest of the class
- groups discussing their ideas and presenting a short talk or a poster
- groups planning an investigation and sharing ideas with the rest of the class
- groups interpreting information in the form of graphs or tables and presenting their findings to others.

Role of Writing Languages

Writing is usually an individual activity, the form and content of writing 'is shaped by the community around us'. Advocates of using writing to help the development of understanding in science emphasise its potential in helping learners to 'make meaning'. Pupils who are asked to write 'in their own words' are expected to use this opportunity to make their own sense of some event or phenomena that they are describing. In practice, however, most experience of this 'expressive' writing is that it often misses the focus of the particular ideas which are to be learned.

There are also those who claim that science is a language of its own and 'cannot be understood in your own words'. This view is that writing in science is a particular genre and that students have to learn how to do it and how particular forms of writing serve the purposes of science. The notion of 'writing frames' developed by Lewis and Wray has been adapted by several schools and local authorities to support writing in science. Research evidence suggests that few pupils are taught these skills. The APU (Assessment of Performance Unit) surveys found that the writing of more than 70% of 11-year-olds was poor when asked to plan a science investigation.

7

ICTs in Libraries

Digital Images

Users of digital images can be divided into two categories: those who create digital images or are involved in their creation through commissioning, managing or perhaps financing the creation; and those who make use of those images as part of their work through, for example, manipulation of the image, study of the subject matter or interest in the digital object itself. Although any system or resource should be developed in light of its end-user, imperatives from 'behind the scenes' can often be more influential; for example, the requirements of legal entities, branding experts or funding bodies. In terms of a preservation process, it is therefore necessary to explore the needs of both sets of users, and to establish the impact that each will have on the other's needs or requirements. Both groups are 'stakeholders' in the strategies, processes and systems needed for preserving digital images.

Perhaps, for ease of reference, the behind-the-scenes participants should be referred to as 'Start-users': the individuals or organisations who contribute to the development, deployment or expansion of the resource to be preserved, or to the preservation system itself. Users of digital images can be defined as two simple groups. There are a number of ways that user groups can be identified to provide a cross section of the UK HE community as relevant to the JISC. They can be considered in respect to both larger scale environments and to smaller, more specific areas of usage. A comprehensive list of content creators that affect the JISC community can be found in State of Art Review, but some of the broad categories are presented here as the basis for subsequent analysis.

The users whose needs must be considered are described here in terms of the HE education sector as well as particular aspects of the collateral environment; for example, users of museums/galleries or staff/students of Further Education institutions. However, usage of images will clearly cover a broad spectrum of different approaches, and it is necessary to think of a 'user' in a number of diverse ways. The following list breaks down the potential users of images in UK education according to several broad and distinct perspectives. Users of online, education-led services:

- JISC-funded collections (e.g. BioMed, AHDS Visual Arts, Education Images Online);
- International collections (e.g. MOMA—New York, PictureAustralia, the Louvre);
- National institutions (e.g. National Gallery, Victoria & Albert Museum, English Heritage);
- Regional institutions (e.g. Glasgow Museums, Manchester Art Gallery);
- Commercial/subscription-based providers (e.g. Bridgeman Art Library, Wellcome Trust);
- Higher Education institute external providers (e.g. Birkbeck, Courtauld Institute).

Users of internal institution provision:

- Intranets
- Institutional repositories
- Virtual Learning Environments (e.g. Blackboard, WebCT)
- Shared drives
- Digital slide libraries

Users of images in different areas of education:

- Non-vocational;
- Lifelong learning;
- Further education;
- Higher education;
- Masters study;
- PhD study;
- Post doctoral research.

Users with different roles:

- Students;
- Researchers;
- Support staff;
- Practitioner;
- Lecturers;
- Managers;
- Librarians.

Users with different learning needs:

- Dyslexia

- Colour blindness
- Physical impairment
- English as a second language

Users with different subject needs:

- Humanities
- Engineering, applied sciences and technology
- Languages, linguistics and literature
- Library and information technology
- Philosophy and Psychology
- Religion and Theology
- Social Sciences, Law and Government

In order to deal with the potential complexity of trying to establish all user needs in the JISC environment relating to the preservation of digital images, four approaches have been taken:

1. Targeted survey with representatives from a cross-section sample of the above groups with an emphasis on talking to users with some level of understanding of digital image preservation needs for their particular area;
2. A non-prescriptive broad survey was made available through AHDS websites and via email lists, to elicit unprompted preservation needs and specialist requirements.;
3. Creation of profiles of archetypal users covering a range of different perspectives and levels of understanding regarding digital image preservation;
4. Desk-top research examining previous work on digital image preservation user needs.

Users' Perspective

The four approaches to identifying user needs have been collated, and an outline of responses, thoughts and ideas is assimilated in the following sections:

Educational Needs

Most users of images in education are primarily interested in their preservation as it relates to teaching, learning and research aims and practices. Many of them, particularly lecturers, use images for presentations and, traditionally, the slide projector has been the main tool of this trade. However, as many digital immigrants are now discovering, there has recently been a significant shift from the traditional approach, exemplified by the fact that well-known slide projector manufacturer, Kodak, announced that production and sales of their machines would end in June 2004, with service and support ceasing in 2011.

In September 2003, the company issued a press release explaining their decision in light of the fact that: "..in recent years, slide projectors have declined in usage, replaced by alternative projection technologies." Although, most users are quickly converting to the new digital display technologies, such as PowerPoint, the dramatic and in some cases unwelcome transition, is a cause of concern when considering preservation issues: users worry that sudden developments in new technology could still render all the current work to preserve digital images obsolete in the not too distant future.

The rapid change in technological approach also stimulates another concern relating to the educational needs behind the preservation of images. This is the notion that pedagogical perspectives have always been subject to change, in response to stimulators such as government edicts, new research and altering social fashions. Consequently, it is possible that any process for preserving digital images today, no matter how technologically stable, will not necessarily be capable of evolving to meet changes in educational needs of the future. One possible implication here is that traditional user views of archives and preservation processes may have to change fundamentally, to a model which can itself adapt to both technological and pedagogical changes, 'on the fly'.

In essence, the management processes and expectations in the user domain may have to 'migrate' just as the digital object must—a switch from "batch processing" to "continuous processing". Whilst such associated concepts as "depreciation" and "lifecycle costing" may be familiar elsewhere, they are new ideas to a sector where resources are traditionally built up over long periods of time and preserved on the shelf, with relatively minimal maintenance, for future students and staff. With such notions comes added complexity, and need for more training and human resources and, inevitably, an increase (or significant change) in costing models.

Subject Distinctions

Consequently, representatives of different subject areas may perceive different values in the process of preserving, and then accessing, digital images. The range covers everything from, as one expert respondent commented: "A broad range, some as pure eye candy to those that are intrinsic to the learning episodes". However, trying to identify such differences proves to be a difficult task. It seems that many apparent difference are simply varying perceptions based on principles, processes and terminology within different disciplines, and they do not directly impact the way an image should be preserved. Most of the different requirements can be met, if digital image preservation processes work to the highest possible technical standards and with a view to preserving the main attributes of an image, as defined below. In essence, there is a lowest common denominator for digital image preservation.

Dissemination/access Preferences

There is only one reason to preserve digital images: so that they are available to people in the future. As the results of the broad survey indicate, to most users of digital images access and metadata are the two top areas of concern regarding preservation.

As is the case with any knowledge source, digital or otherwise, appropriate indexing or cataloguing of the resources is imperative. In a digital information system, whether it be for short or long term access, such 'descriptions' of the object are held in metadata fields. This is particularly relevant for the archiving of, and subsequent access to images, since by virtue of their visual nature, they commonly travel without any intrinsic (textual) information. Without understandable metadata, there is significant risk that the future will produce millions of images that will be unsearchable, unidentifiable and unusable.

These mostly relate to the difficulties of preserving terminology, with the images, that will ensure their usability and re-usability across a vast range of potential users, in an infinite number of ways and into an unknown future. Two areas of terminology need to be considered:

i) *Content-specific terminology*: To enable different users to successfully access material in the future, different considerations need to be given to differing approaches. Usually this involves creating metadata for particular images based on the subject area within which that image sits. This is achieved through the use of specific metadata schemas. However, user practices change, and in turn, so can the terminology employed to find images. If the user terminology alters over time then the usefulness of the preserved images, with their terminology based on a fixed point, will diminish. Lehman's Laws (relating to software evolution) all point to the need to accept change as intrinsic to the development of any system. In particular, his first law states, "in accord with universal experience, that a system must be continually adapted else it becomes progressively less satisfactory". This is as true of the metadata and other descriptive terminology employed as it is of the objects or the system itself.

ii) *Technology-driven terminology*: Most users are concerned with achieving educational aims and, consequently, have little need (or desire) to understand mega-pixels, bitstreams or emulation techniques. As the digital preservation project at the British Library found out, it is important to users that jargonis kept to the necessary only. Particularly when designing systems and processes that are to be understood in the future, any terms used need to be either explained as part of the process (e.g. through glossaries or thesauri) and/or, where possible, presented in as plain a language as possible. This is also important because of the fact that different people will read different meanings into such terms; for example, in the Cedars project, it was noted that, "the relative novelty of digital preservation as an issue for libraries, and the fact that expertise in this area resides in other sectors (e.g. electronic records management) means that defining what we mean by specific terms is sometimes contentious. Where librarians, archivists, records managers and computing technologists assemble, the term "archive" can (and does) mean very different things."

Both of the above issues indicate a need for acceptance that terminology within a preservation system needs to be considered extremely carefully, else it may reduce the success with which users will be able to access the material within. However, in terms of access to all users, preservation systems need to also consider the important issues of accessibility for disadvantaged users. Images pose a particular problem for some users, particularly, for example, those with visual impairments, and it is essential that a system for providing long term access is fully compliant with guidelines for accessibility (e.g. W3C) both now and in the future. It may be that the standards, approaches and technologies of the future permit greater accessibility to digital images for a wider range of users, and a preservation system must be equipped to accommodate such change.

Preservation of Digital Images

Quality of image

The quality of images is generally seen as an important issue for most users. However, the definition of quality itself is open to a number of different interpretations when discussing the attributes most significant in a preservation process. Nonetheless, most quality issues can be described in one of two ways:

- Whether the content is sufficient for the task. This qualitative, and usually subjective, value is based on things such as the subject matter itself: whether the digital image offers a good representation of its subject; and whether it fits in with the views, tastes and current needs of the user. Such issues have long been applicable to pictorial representations and do not seem to alter significantly when addressed to digital images.

– Whether the object itself is good enough for the task. Although this issue can also be subjective, its most significant elements relate to more technical attributes; for example, the level of detail (LoD), colour depth, pixilation or resolution, and are based on an assumption that the content is satisfactory

In both cases, the overriding factor in user decisions about quality is fitness for purpose. Different users will have very different ideas about what constitutes quality in either sense. In terms of the quality of the object, again different users can have very different definitions of fitness for their purpose; for example, a history tutor talking about Winston Churchill to an FE class may only require a 72dpi copy of a grainy, black and white photograph to illustrate his/her talk, whereas a geology researcher trying to identify features on aerial photographs may require very high definition, high resolution images to be sure of his/her findings.

Unfortunately, one issue that cannot be overcome by this approach is the fact that, as display mechanisms improve, today's very high quality image will, by tomorrow's standards, be of an increasingly poorer quality. There is a widespread belief among many user communities that quality of digital images can be defined in terms of numbers of pixels; an image that is 2000 pixels across and 300dpi, is considered a 'good quality' image. What is less understood is that, for preservation purposes, this is only a relative measurement.

In ten years time, such an image will probably be considered 'poor quality', particularly as display mechanisms improve. The solution to this dilemma, in defining possible user needs of future communities, may lie in Nicholas Negroponte's observations on the early development of digital television screens. He emphasised that fact that scalability is the key to ensuring digital growth and that "when people argue over the number of scan lines, the frame rate, or the aspect ratio of television in the future, one can rest assured they are discussing the most irrelevant pieces of the puzzle." He follows up this assertion by stating that the future of all digital media will not be to do with these sorts of erroneous 'standards': "it will be nothing but a bit stream."

The quality of an image should relate to its fitness of purpose; no-one judges the quality of a television programme according to the number of lines on the screen. However, amongst the concerns there is also some confidence in the education community. Nonetheless, many users do worry about just what is being preserved, though most would probably agree that, in terms of preservation processes, it is safe to assume that preserving the highest available quality of object, in as many respects as is possible, is the best way to serve the future needs of users of digital images. The following points help to determine exactly what constitutes a 'good quality' image.

Selection procedure

Arguably more important than 'pixel quality' to many users of images, is ensuring that the right images are chosen for preservation in the first place. Sadly, not all digital images that are created today will be saved for tomorrow, and, although there are arguments for a cover-all approach, there are a number of advantages to the eventual users in a more critical selection procedure. The National Library of Australia, in its own plans to digitise material, point out that, not only has this been the normal case for non-digital material, but, selecting a limited number of items to be preserved enables creators to devote more time to: inject quality control into the collecting process; negotiate explicit access rights; develop relationships with creators and publishers; maintain working knowledge of changing technological features and file formats; realistically record metadata for future preservation decisions; and, realistically commit to maintaining access to the material.

Nonetheless, such an approach does provoke questions about just how such a process will take place. For example, it is currently very difficult to maintain the integral structure of a website in any way that is guaranteed to survive into the future. This means that, simply because of 'technical' impediments, many potential valuable websites will vanish. This sort of selection is, of course, far from ideal for the integrity of preserving educational material for future generations. Beyond that, users worry that decisions will be made on the grounds of lack of perceived quality (in pixel terms), or lack of support at departmental, institutional or National level because of political or funding criteria rather than understanding of educational need.

Provenance

For end-users of images in an educational environment, one of the most important factors is being able to establish the reliability, authenticity and authentication of the source from which a reference is taken, whether that be a textual reference or an image. This is increasingly difficult in the free-flowing hypertext world and users believe that mechanisms and processes for attributing provenance to digital objects is an extremely important factor in their future usability. Across the broad scope of the UK education community, there are inevitably many ways that such provenance can be defined.

But a Nancy Brodie cites a number of different views surrounding the authentication issue; for example "definition and preservation of those features of an information object that distinguish it as a whole and singular work", or "Authentication provides verification that a digital object is what it purports to be and contains the contents that the author/creator or publisher originally intended." She sums up by saying that most definitions "have in common an understanding that authentication is a process which allows future users to determine the authenticity of objects or proves the authenticity of objects", and that there will be different levels of authenticity for different communities as well as different levels of authentication.

Currently, much of the UK education sector uses Athens as an authentication firewall, and most users tend to assume that, if an information source lies behind it, it is probably of a reasonably safe form to be used in an educational context. But, as more and more digital images become available, perhaps via a VLE or institutional repository, such confidence in the integrity and authenticity of the object is diminishing. Users are concerned that, if images are to be preserved, how will their integrity or authenticity, their provenance, be preserved with them.

Permissions and copyright

Permissions and copyright, and other IPR issues, have been causing difficulties for users of images from the outset of the digital age. This is particularly so in education, where there is an understanding of, and willingness to meet the principles behind such issues. The education community, whilst believing that staff and students should have free and open access to the images they need, also understands the need to ensure that the legitimate rights of the creator or owner are fully protected. This sets up something of a conflict that is hard to resolve; for example, in the arts and medical world, the rights of many images are necessarily restrictive, yet these same images can be of fundamental importance for the teaching of those disciplines.

This issue is exacerbated when considerations are given to preservation and the longevity of permissions needed to ensure future access, particularly given that definitions of 'educational usage' will almost certainly change over time, and completely new needs will emerge that may be outside the permissions associated with the image. Nonetheless, issues for users regarding copyright of images preserved for long periods of time are, inevitably, similar to the issues of using digital images in general. The key to copyright or IPR issues regarding long term access can be summed up in two ways: all images within a preservation system must have complete permission clearance, for any current or possible future use, in perpetuity; or, there must be a built in facility or process that enables permissions to be revisited in response to user needs.

Formats

Formats do appear, on the surface to be of importance to users. Most people seem to accept that new formats will come along and, on the whole, this is not seen as a problem; there is an implicit assumption, based on most people's experiences of digital technologies, that the new formats will be an improvement on the current, and that they will most likely be backward compatible—at least for as long as is necessary for content to be migrated forward in a suitable state.

However, as with the technical issues of migration, whether the right components travel to the next format is dependant on the process used, the new format itself, descriptions added later and, of course, how much human intervention is applied. Furthermore, librarians, archivists and other conservators of analogue resources are, perhaps rightly, concerned that in the digital era format and media are increasingly hard to separate. Consequently, the image format which might once have been described according to its media type (e.g. photographic negative), is now simply a binary code viewable only on a machine capable of understanding the particular variation of ones and zeros.

As such the future of digital media does have an intrinsic difference to its analogue forebears: images preserved on paper, glass plate or even the humble thirty-five millimetre slide already have a proven track record and, in fact, still exist, where they have been properly preserved. Whereas, in the digital arena, much material has already been lost to the countless piles of 3", 3.5", 5", 8" disks and, as presentation and storage formats continue to evolve, it is a fair assumption that many digital images will be 'forgotten'. As far as most user needs are concerned, it would seem that factors relating to format will ultimately be governed by the non-technical aspects of image quality, provenance and permissions and copyright, as identified above.

Properties of Digital Images

File formats continue to evolve, becoming more complex as

revised software versions add new features and functionality. It is not uncommon for software enhancements to render files generated by earlier versions unreadable. The threat to aging digital information has surpassed the danger of unstable media or obsolete hardware, the most pressing problems confronting managers of digital repositories are data format and software obsolescence.

File (or data) formats define the rules used by application software to convert bits (the fundamental unit of digital data) into meaningful information that can be viewed and manipulated by a user. Most application software developers produce file format documentation for the formats they design and develop. Based on the availability and stability of the format specification, file formats can be classified as proprietary, open or standard formats. Proprietary file formats are not public and are developed and maintained by software producers. Larger software producers may sometimes publish their format specifications (PAS—Publicly Available Specification) or several firms may join together in a consortium to define interface standards so that they can develop mutually compatible products. These are called open or public file formats.

Some file formats are developed to become international standards (standard file formats) which are then public and fixed or stable until the next release of the standard. It is not unusual that software companies produce their own modified, proprietary, versions of standard file formats—these will be based on standards, but will have extensions that are proprietary and generally not public (e.g., Microsoft's version of XML). Many proprietary formats are, nevertheless, widely used and provide extensive compatibility with application software—these formats are often classified as de facto standards. Successful and cheap long-term preservation of a digital file depends on the openness, level of standardisation and compatibility with other software products of the file format.

Without a format specification the vital rendering tools that enable the use of digital files over longer time cannot be developed. Reverse engineering of software or the digital objects themselves can provide some answers, although legal constraints may well prevent this kind of action. Even where reverse engineering is possible, without any file format documentation, the process is likely to be too laborious and expensive.

The preservation risks associated with file formats are mostly related to loss of data and cost. Both migration and emulation—the two best digital preservation strategies currently in use—rely on file format specification being known and accurate. If it is not, the preservation strategies risk introducing distortion, loss of quality or data, or not being able to render the file usable at all. The risk management of file formats for preservation has to account for all these considerations.

Vector Graphics

A vector image is created 'on-the-fly' either by plotting objects defined in a database or some other form of structured data, or by executing a sequence of drawing instructions. The image is rendered by software to a raster device such as a computer monitor or a printer. Vector graphics data are used in many drawing and illustration packages, CAD programs, most 3D modelling and animation programs, and coordinate based mapping applications. They are also often used in page layout and plotting situations. The definitions of scalable fonts available for printers and windowed computer environments also consist of vector data although these would not normally be considered as images. Vector data may be referenced according to fixed, arbitrary or relative coordinate systems.

Fixed coordinate systems are generally used by illustration and drawing packages with the coordinate system usually mapping to a page. CAD packages use arbitrary coordinate systems that suit the data. The basic unit of the coordinate system can be as small as an Angstrom unit or as large as a light year, and objects can exist anywhere within the limits of the numeric precision used to store the coordinates values (essentially from minus to plus infinity). Relative coordinate systems are used where only the relationships between the elements of the image are significant, for example in molecular diagrams, and also by some metafile formats which just need to know how far and in what direction to draw a line or curve from the current drawing position.

Coordinate systems can theoretically have any number of dimensions but normally two or three are used. The amount of descriptive information held in a vector data file varies between applications. Usually CAD files fully describe geometrical objects (e.g. lines, polygons, ellipses) and their attributes (e.g. colour, line type) along with their position and extrusion in two- or three-dimensional space. In certain applications the type of the objects is known and only their absolute or relative positions need to be defined as, for example, with GIS data where the objects are polygons (points and lines can be considered as simple polygons) and only lists of vertices need to be stored.

Similarly with molecular or crystallographic data only the details of the chemical bonds needs to be stored as the rendering program can supply the atoms and representations of the bonds between them. A consequence of storing the image information as vector data is that the coordinate system of the image must be mathematically transformed to map it to that of the target device. This transformation generally requires one or more of translation, scaling and rotation. As a result it is a simple matter to apply any level of zoom, select any part of the image to display and apply arbitrary rotations without loss of image quality by manipulating parameters in the transform. Vector graphics formats often store bitmap information. The bitmap graphic is generally stored as a simple rectangle having a complex fill (i.e. a raster image is embedded within a vector graphic).

Properties of vector images

Significant properties of vector images differ depending on the general application and on the specific purpose of the data. A large array of different technologies and applications produce vector graphics with a consequence that the following guidelines focus on the generic issues. In some cases more specific information is available in the AHDS Guides to Good Practice series including guides to CAD, GIS, Geophysics, Remote Sensing and Virtual Reality.

File formats: The file format determines which software is able to render the content to an output device. There is a degree of interoperability between software and file formats for given application types through the agreement and use of standards. These may range from agreement amongst software vendors to support open source export or exchange formats to the increasing support for XML within applications. In being ASCII based the latter provides an ideal basis for long-term preservation.

Many proprietary vector graphics software packages use binary formats natively which can be problematic even when the format is documented as an open standard in that archiving in the long term involves version migration as the format evolves. Fortunately, many software packages (but by no means all) provide export facilities as ASCII text which as already noted is the ultimate preservation format.

Scale: In CAD and GIS files the creator decides on the basic unit of measurement. For geographic data this will usually be a metre, for architectural data either a millimetre or, in the U.S., a foot. It is important that the value of the basic unit is documented. Crystallographic and molecular data files fix the basic unit as being an angstrom. Scale is normally irrelevant in illustration files as the image is intended to fit on a page.

Precision and accuracy: The precision of the data in vector images is dependant on the discipline from which the data is drawn. Geospatial CAD and GIS data, when collected by survey, are likely to have been collected at a precision greater than necessary. Modern survey equipment usually works to a precision of a few millimetres whereas geographic data seldom requires better then a metre precision. Architectural drawings are generally drawn to a precision of a millimetre. Engineering data often requires sub-millimetre precision. The accuracy of the data is, in many cases, important, and may even be critical in engineering drawings. In this case there should be a statement specifying the reliability of the data, particularly if the data has been modified from its original format (e.g. through coordinate transformation).

Geographical coordinate systems: Geographical coordinates can be expressed as angles of longitude and latitude or within a national or international planar Cartesian coordinate system. The former locates features on the globe whilst the latter within a map projection. Because maps are a two-dimensional representation in part of something spherical, distortion is generally a problem. Consequently, to reduce distortion coverage of large areas tends to be achieved through a large number of map projections covering smaller areas. Locations can also be covered by multiple projections.

GIS files and CAD files depicting geography are frequently geo-referenced to a particular map projection. In such cases it is vital that the coordinate system or map projection the data conforms to is fully documented. Clearly this is not the case for arbitrary or relatively referenced vector data.

Geometry: The most significant content of CAD files is the geometry; the disposition of lines, points, text, and other simple or complex drawing objects in the two- or threedimensional space of the model. For topographic data in GIS files it is the coordinate location of spatial units and what they are (i.e. points, lines or polygons) that is important. Other packages producing vector data rely on regularly collected point data in the form of a grid and thus have a fixed geometry.

Objects and their relationships: Crystallographic and molecular data define the atoms making up a compound and also the relationships between each atom as a description of the atomic bonds.

Conventions: Extra meaning can be given to objects in CAD files through the use of layers, colours, line weights and line types and also their incorporation into groups or blocks. These can be used to classify objects into groups or different types. GIS applications may use colour coding to represent different categories of information. Both CAD and

GIS support layers. For example, one GIS layer may contain data pertaining to road systems whilst another might represent river systems. Layers can be viewed independently or superimposed. One potential problem area relates to invisible material included within layers (possibly switched off or frozen, etc). These can be purged unless there are clear reasons for retention. As such, conventions convey meaning and it is important that they are fully documented.

Associated data: Most CAD packages allow external data to be linked to drawings. These may be supplied with the software package, e.g. line styles and symbol libraries, or may be custom material. The latter can be user-defined line styles, symbols, bitmap images, or complete drawings, generally incorporated as blocks. Similarly some molecular formats have associated files. The absence of any such external data may not be obvious to a re-user and may substantially degrade the value of the image. Generally speaking vector image formats concerned with geographical survey (geophysical, lidar, marine, etc) and a number of GIS formats can have associated non-geometrical data (attribute data).

It is also possible to link non-geometrical data to many CAD file formats giving such files basic GIS functionality. CAD files may have databases holding data describing physical characteristics of objects or materials in the model or drawing or, particularly for architectural drawings, part identifications and costs for repeated objects allowing ordering information or bills of materials to be calculated. Illustrations are frequently associated with some text in an associated text document. In the absence of this text the image may be meaningless. Clearly the existence of associated data needs to be recorded and the data maintained as part of any long-term preservation strategy

Methodology: The methodology used in collecting survey and molecular data has substantial implications for accuracy and interpretation. Thus a GIS survey carried out using a total station EDM with an accuracy measured in millimetres is more trustworthy than one carried out using 30m tapes and triangulation, X-ray diffraction studies on a molecule may lead to a different interpretation than does nuclear magnetic resonance.

Risk assessment in vector graphics

Many vector graphics software packages generate binary files which can be problematic for longer term preservation. Fortunately many, but not all, allow for export as structured ASCII text which is generally accepted as being the most stable of formats. An ASCII export is not enough in itself as its meaning has to be openly documented. Formats that either export or natively use ASCII including XML are inherently stable. In general if long-term preservation is an issue software packages that only support binary should be avoided. The following commonly used technologies and formats therein are recognised as having specific problems.

PostScript and its variants: PDF appears to be subsuming other PostScript formats. Adobe have released the documentation for this popular format as an open standardbut the preservation of PDF files has always been an issue. A frequently used solution is to capture each page of a PDF in an alternative format such as a raster format such as tiff. Recently, an international standard, ISO 19005-1, has been agreed for the long term preservation of PDF files. PDF-A (for archive) is based on version 1.4 of the PDF format but is constrained in that, for example, executables including use of JavaScript are not allowed, fonts must be embedded and encryption is prohibited. That a PDF file will still contain executable instructions (PostScript) there are still questions about its suitability as a preservation format.

Computer Aided Design (CAD): The text-based version of DXF format used for exchanging files between CAD (Computer Aided Design) packages is maintained by the major CAD software vendor, AutoDesk, and reflects the latest version of their package AutoCAD. AutoDesk have not released documentation about changes in recent versions of AutoCAD which means other vendors cannot support them. In short it is no longer an open standard. Consequently, the only realistic way of preserving AutoCAD drawings is through version migration. Purchasing and migrating through successive versions can be a very expensive procedure in terms of time as well as financial outlay.

Geographic Information Systems (GIS): The major GIS software vendors, ESRI and MapInfo provide import and export routines for the interchange of data. The lack of an open standard has led to ESRI formats being accepted as / de facto/ standards amongst users. Recently ESRI have introduced add-on modules for their ArcGIS and ArcIMS packages which provide support for XML based open standards; Web Map Server (WMS) and Geography Markup Language (GML) and hence compliance to the Open Geospatial Consortium (OGC) standard. A JISC funded Interoperability Demonstrator Project is currently investigating the use of these standards.

Chemical and Molecular formats: The emergence of CML should cater for such formats.

Raster Images

The raster image is the most common category of image created and used within digitisation projects, and delivered over the Internet. All scanners and digital cameras produce raster images and most output devices (print and screen) also use them. Raster images take the form of a grid or matrix, whose pattern becomes easily visible as the image is magnified. Each square or picture element (pixel) within the matrix occupies a unique position and can be edited separately. Each pixel stores colour information and the pixels taken in their entirety make up the image.

Internally, a raster image's coding typically includes a header describing the structure of the file followed by a series of values, each describing the colour of the individual pixels. Since raster images record information for each pixel, their file size can be relatively large. For an uncompressed raster image, the file size will be directly related to its pixel dimensions (spatial resolution) and the extent of the colour information recorded for each pixel (its colour resolution or 'bit-depth'). Although most raster file formats are similar in structure, they can be distinguished by the amount of information they record per pixel (i.e. their bit-depth), the methods used to record their code more efficiently (their compression), and the additional functionality they offer (e.g. transparency layers, colour management or metadata support). They can also be divided into open formats and proprietary formats.

The main defining features of a raster image are: The file format of the image relates to the type of computer code that is used to structure the raster image. There are many choices for the type of format to choose for raster images. Different file formats offer differing levels of compatibility and compression. For archival purposes non-proprietary formats without compression are best.

Resolution: The resolution of an image concerns the number of pixels held within the digital file, and is measured in pixels per inch (ppi). The more pixels stored per inch, the greater the density of the colour information, and therefore the greater the detail evident in the image. The appropriateness of the resolution chosen depends on the intended purpose of the digital image. However, note that resolution or ppi is only an indicator of image size, and therefore 'quality', when we know the dimensions of the original analogue object.

For example, scanning an A4 document (9 × 12 inches) at 300 ppi will produce a digital image that is 2700 pixels x 3600 pixels (the dimensions of the original multiplied by the ppi). Scanning a postage stamp that is 1 inch x 1 inch in size, will produce a digital image that is 300 pixels x 300 pixels. Both these images are scanned at the same 300ppi resolution, but produce vastly different sized digital images. A more accurate way to refer to the size of a raster image therefore is to use its pixel dimensions.

Bit Depth: Bit-depth refers to the amount of colour information held with each individual pixel. In a greyscale image there are usually 8 'bits' of information in each pixel, in a colour image 24 bits are standard, although some software will scan at 48 bit. The number of bits of information held in a raster image also impacts on file size.

Colour Space: The colour space of an image refers to the method of working with colour based on colour models. The most common colour models are bitonal, grayscale, Indexed colour, RGB and CMYK. The bitonal mode uses only two colour values, black and white, to display images. The grayscale mode offers 256 shades of grey that range from white to black. Indexed colour is the limited palette of 216 colours that web designers are able to use which display on both Macintoshes and PCs.

It is more usual to work in RGB and then only convert to Index colour mode if you think it will really effect your users e.g. if a logo has to display as a certain shade of red. Computer monitors and TV screens use the RGB model to display a mixture of red, green and blue colour values. The CMYK model refers to the printing colours of cyan, magenta, yellow and black. The colour model effects the file size of the image, since the more bits and bytes, the larger the file size. Images with only black or white pixels (bitonal—1 bit per colour channel) will therefore have the smallest file sizes, grayscale images quite small file sizes (8 bits per colour channel) whereas RGB images with 24-bits (8 bits per colour channel) or more will have much bigger file sizes.

Another issue to consider is that it can be difficult to convert from RGB to CMYK. This is normally done when you need a commercial company to print an image for you. When you convert to CMYK you need to be aware of the 'gamut'. The term gamut refers to the range of colours that the combination of CMYK inks print. Some colours may be 'out of gamut' and therefore can't be printed accurately. This can be resolved with certain programmes, such as PhotoShop, that provide an 'out of gamut' warning, and give you options to replace a colour with one that is in the gamut. It is best to work in RGB and then keep a copy as RGB and convert another copy to CMYK if needed for printing purposes.

Raster image preservation file formats

The stable long term raster image preservation file formats—TIFF, PNG, JPG2000 and DNG, giving information on origins, characteristics, suitability and any potential shortfalls both now and into the future. These are described below.

TIFF: Baseline TIFF revision 6 is a recommended file format for raster image preservation. No compression or additional functionality, available in some other format revisions, should be used. Having been the 'defacto' standard for digital image preservation for the past ten years with widespread industry and software support, it is expected to remain an acceptable preservation format for the foreseeable future.

JPEG2000: JPEG2000 is, in its current form, an acceptable preservation standard. It has the advantage of ISO status, is non-proprietary and has some excellent functionality. However at time of writing the format falls short of full recommendation. This is mainly due to relatively slow take up among industry and leading software and web browser developers. Although difficult to predict, the likelihood, indeed the hope, is that over time this support will be forthcoming and JPEG2000 will achieve fully recommended preservation format status.

PNG: To some extent PNG is in the same position as JPEG2000 above, in that it is an acceptable preservation format but falls short, at time of writing, of fully recommended status. It is an open standard with W3C support and, as of 2003, ISO status. The main caveats to full recommendation are lack of browser support (Internet Explorer for Windows being the main culprit), and simultaneously a lack of full software support among some vendors, and some additions to the format made by others. As with TIFF above, only baseline versions should be used for image preservation. And as with JPEG2000 above, the hope is that the lack of support will be overcome over time, and PNG will achieve fully recommended status.

DNG: It is a new addition to the range of possibilities, so is untested in its wider application, and may be limited in use to images created using one shot digital cameras. It is also proprietary, although the same caveat applies also to TIFF. Furthermore, as DNG is an Adobe developed format there is a strong possibility that wider software support will be forthcoming in the next few years, and the format's 'not recommended' status may need to be revisited.

METHODS OF PRESERVATION

The great difficulty anyone trying to undertake preservation of digital content will encounter is the lack of practical advice, and of robust tools and mature techniques for digital preservation. A number of digital preservation strategies have been proposed, but there is no definitive approach to the problem of maintaining digital content across multiple generations of technology. Unfortunately, information on the likely costs, possible limitations and long-term sustainability of different strategies is still quite limited—partly for the very valid reason that no one has yet had the time to gain the experience needed to answer these questions. Few organisations with digital preservation responsibilities appear to have yet fully developed their policies in this area.

It is unwise to commit to a course of action before its consequences are clear, nevertheless it is equally important that organisations which make some claim to preserve digital resources should declare to their stakeholders what they can do to achieve this goal at the present time. Decisions about preservation methods might usefully take into account the following three-tiered understanding of digital preservation:

- Preservation of the bit stream (basic sequences of binary digits) that ultimately represent the information stored in any digital resource

- Preservation of the information content (words, images, sounds etc.) stored as bits and defined by a logical data model, embodied in a file or media format
- Preservation of the experience (speed, layout, display device, input device characteristics etc.) of interacting with the information content

Techniques for achieving the first of these objectives are well understood and include environmentally controlled storage, data replication, backup, and media refreshment. In the OAIS model, much of this activity falls into the archival storage function. The second and third objectives present a far greater challenge. Binary data remains useful only for as long as it can be correctly rendered (displayed, played-back, interacted with) into meaningful content such as text, images and video clips. The process of rendering is performed by a complex mix of hardware and software, which is subject to rapid obsolescence.

As a rule of thumb, it is reasonable to predict that current hardware and software will be able to correctly render a file for around ten years after its creation. By the end of this period, repositories need to have adopted a more active preservation strategy than simply preserving the bit stream of the file if they are to maintain access to information content held in the file. Either old data must be altered to operate in a new technical environment (migration, format standardisation) or the new environment must be modified so that it can render the old data (emulation, virtual computers). Within these two broad approaches there are many different techniques.

Bitstream Preservation

This simply involves retaining the original data as a single sequence of binary digits (bits), i.e. the original data in an uninterpreted state. Bitstreams may be preserved in two ways: either as the original file in the data format as received, e.g. An MS Word document, a TIFF image, a plaintext file etc.; or in a normalised bitstream format, e.g. as a sequence of bits contained inside XML wrappers. Bitstream preservation is widely viewed as a form of 'insurance' in that it allows for the possibility of using future techniques for making content accessible. Moreover, it is an additional form of data backup. It is hard to see that the first method offers any real advantages over the second.

In either case metadata is needed to make sense of the file. Using the first method, the metadata would need to be kept separately but associated with the data content, perhaps, for example, in a separate METS file. The second method has the advantage that metadata about the file and its format can be included within the XML wrappers surrounding the content bitstream and is thus always kept with the associated content data. The second method is to be preferred.

Technology Preservation

Technology preservation is an attempt to ensure the usability of digital resources over time by preserving and maintaining software (applications and operating systems) hardware, essentially creating an IT museum. This may be a useful shortterm solution but costs in terms of the maintenance and storage of equipment makes it prohibitive for any sustained strategy. As an example, AHDS Archaeology maintains a small 'computer museum' but 'exhibits' are intended to facilitate data recovery, not time-based access to source files, and have been used in earnest for recovery purposes.

Data is moved into stable open formats and thus into a format migration strategy. At one stage the museum contained two working Amstrad computers but both of these have now failed and are not able to be repaired. A hardware preservation strategy would fail in the same way, without the expenditure of large sums of money to ensure that technologists with appropriate skills are always available. This approach cannot be regarded as viable.

Migration

Migration as a preservation term can be used to describe both file format migration and media migration. Media migration is more often known as 'refreshment' and is necessary to ensure that data is not lost through media degradation over time. The lifetime of media must be estimated and migration to new media undertaken before the threshold is reached. Today there is a move toward storage on hard disk with multiple disk or tape backups. Integrity between versions is maintained through the use of fixity or checksum values as with the OAIS reference model. Refreshment is an essential activity in any preservation programme, but does not in itself ensure data preservation.

File format migration is used to ensure the accessibility of a digital object when the software it depends on becomes obsolete or unusable. It can involve conversion of digital objects from one file format to another format, for example from Word 98 to Word 2000, from Word 2000 to Adobe's Portable Document Format (PDF), or from GIF to PNG. Some attributes of the digital object may be lost during the conversion process, so the experience may not be equivalent after migration.

The level of data loss through migration depends on the number of preservation treatments applied to the record, the choice of process, the new data format, the level of human intervention and post-migration descriptive work. Migration as an approach has a number of variations. The traditional technique is to migrate file formats to newer versions of the same format as the earlier versions approach complete obsolescence, eg Word 95 to Word 98 to Word 2000. This method requires migration at as late a stage in the life of the digital format as possible.

A second migration technique involves migrating digital objects to limited range of standard formats at the time they are ingested by a digital repository. This involves fewer overall migrations but still requires the migration of the standard formats as existing versions of those formats become obsolete. A third technique depends on the migration of all file formats to a standardised file format which is chosen for its presumed longevity as a digital format, eg XML. This migration technique is often referred to as 'normalisation'.

Emulation Technique

Emulation is a technique often proposed as a solution to the hardware/software obsolescence problem. Put simply, emulation involves the development of software to replicate the behaviour of obsolete processes (such as hardware configurations or operating systems) on current hardware. Emulation thus aims to recreate part of the original process that interprets the data to produce a modern rendering of the original performance. Much emulation work is motivated by a belief that the original 'look and feel' of a digital resource must be maintained forever. 'Look and feel' includes the content of the record, but also tangible aspects of the presentation of the content, such as colour, layout, and functionality.

However, it has been pointed out by a number of commentators that "traditionally, preserving things meant keeping them unchanged; however ... if we hold on to digital information without modifications, accessing the information will become increasingly more difficult, if not impossible. The major problem with emulation is that it requires not only the retention of all relevant software applications (i.e. One for every type of file format being preserved), but also the coding of an emulator for every hardware and operating system in use. As well, the whole issue of the significance of the original 'look and feel' is a discussion studiously avoided by proponents of the emulation approach, but is assumed to be of prime importance.

Many people state that recreation of the original experience is of prime importance for digital preservation yet there is little or no quantitative evidence to back this up, and the position is neither a given nor unarguable. It remains little discussed by proponents of emulation, however, but is an important underpinning/justification of this approach and needs to be debated widely.

Migration on request

Conceived by the CEDARS project, migration on request confusingly promotes emulation as a preservation strategy. One of its chief developers says of CEDARS: "Original objects are maintained and preserved in addition to a migration tool which runs on a current computing platform. This would be employed by users to convert the original bytestream of the object they want to use into a current format". A separate migration tool would be needed for each data format ingested by the repository and these would need to be maintained over time, ie. re-coded to cope with operating system and hardware changes.

As well, this approach requires the development and maintenance of rendering tools so the migrated object can be viewed. Again, a separate rendering tool would be needed for each data format and these also would need to be updated as operating system and hardware changed. Software development times suggest that the rendering tools will need to be developed at the same time as the migrating tools so they are on hand to allow a migrated object to be usable at time of migration. The sustainability of such an approach is questionable. Thus, the original object is maintained and the migration tool or emulator is migrated as computer platforms change. This is seen by the CEDARS team as more practical and cost efficient than the original model proposed by Rothenberg where, because of the expense, emulators were to be developed only when necessary.

In the latter case a huge technological gap could build up, but the effort involved in migrating a tool from one version to the next as platform changes occur should be minimal. Clearly, however, this approach would require an ever increasing number of migration tools as software versions and formats increase. There is the further issue of who is going to create, migrate and maintain a repository of the tools. It seems unlikely that individual repositories could sustain such an approach without a large community of implementers of migration on request to call on for sharing of migration and rendering tools.

Universal virtual computer

A development related to emulation as a preservation

strategy is the so-called 'universal virtual computer' (UVC). This concept was proposed in 2000 by Raymond Lorie of IBM, in research paper written for IBM, and later published more widely in an article in RLG DigiNews. In brief, the UVC is a virtual representation of a simplified computer that will run on any existing hardware platform. Its appeal seemingly lies in the fact that problems of hardware and software obsolescence become irrelevant, and digital objects can be retained in their original format. It is said by its proponents to have the advantages of both the emulation approach and the format migration approach, with none of the disadvantages.

The only implementation of this concept is at the Netherlands Koninklijke Bibliotheek (KB) where a test implementation has been developed for preserving digital images (in fact PDF files, each of which is manifested as a sequence of JPEG files). In this, the only real world application of the concept, it becomes clear that there is a large software development and maintenance load on implementers. In order to preserve JPEG images today the KB needs the UVC emulator, a format decoder (and will need one for each format being preserved), a logical data scheme, an equivalent of a document type definition or DTD, (again it will need one for each format), and a viewer that allows viewing of the decoded file.

To access the file in the future the KB will also need to develop a UVC emulator for every hardware/software configuration on which the file will be accessed throughout its useable life. The approach may have some worth, and the KB test implementation is regarded by them as demonstrating "the only method so far that guarantees long-term accessibility of PDF files". However, this is a sweeping statement which is not based on their own experience and which, in any case, can hardly be shown to be accurate except by the passage of time (and it is only a year since the original project finished). The KB implementation itself shows the problems of the UVC approach.

It was set up to as a solution for preserving PDF files, but both KB and IBM found that developing a decoder for PDF was too difficult and complex a task to be completed during the life of the project. Instead, the PDF files were migrated to JPEG—a jpeg image for every individual page in each PDF file—and the JPEG files are preserved as the preservation version of the PDF files. The KB admits that "some of the original aspects of PDF publications are lost when using this method", which would seem to compromise the aim of the project "to preserve the original object".

As well, comparisons of this approach with others in the KB document display a peculiar blind spot in advocates of the UVC: an inability to recognise that migration is not a single technique. It seems likely that the software development burden, as well as issues around the complexity of developing decoders mitigates against the use of this approach in all except the most well-off or financially secure organisations, or those with an extremely limited (and relatively simple) range of file formats being ingested.

8

Confidence Building in ICT Education

The relationships between 'monitoring and evaluation' and 'capacity building and management' are crucial for the successful implementation of technology enhanced learning programmes in three specific ways.

First, it is essential for monitoring and evaluation activities to be well-managed and led so that they can be used effectively for the improvement of technology enhanced educational programmes. Those involved in monitoring and evaluation likewise need to be well trained so that they can deliver sensitive and appropriate recommendations.

Second, monitoring and evaluation have a direct impact on capacity building and management. Used effectively, monitoring and evaluation provide a key mechanism to enable those involved in both formal and informal educational systems to improve their practices.

Third, capacity building and management activities themselves need to be monitored, so that their role in delivering technology enhanced learning can be better understood and enhanced.

Despite this importance, policy makers and practitioners have rarely sufficiently considered the complexities associated with the interactions between these core elements of e-learning strategies. Academic studies have been little better. Cox et al. in their comprehensive review of the research literature on ICT and attainment thus only mention 'management' twice, and fail to mention capacity building at all!

The introduction of ICTs into learning environments, be they in schools, universities, adult learning centres or the workplace, requires inspirational leadership and skilful change management expertise. This is not just a matter of head teachers or Chief Executive Officers (CEOs) being committed to the process, but rather reflects a need for everyone involved to understand the implications of the changes being made, and to feel able to contribute to the processes. Capacity building and management go hand in hand; everyone needs to be trained appropriately, and the processes require careful management.

Appropriate management skills are insufficient by themselves to deliver effective e-learning programmes. It is essential for everyone involved to understand the true potential of ICT to transform learning experiences. Far too often computers have been put into schools with insufficient attention being paid to the ways in which teachers will use them. One of the fundamental lessons to be learnt from European, North American and Australian experiences over the last 20 years has been that those responsible for helping people learn must be confident in the appropriate use of new technologies if the process is to be successful. Introducing new technologies into places of learning should involve a fundamental shift whereby the role of teachers becomes less didactic and more that of facilitating individual learning processes.

For monitoring and evaluation to be effective, all participants in the learning process need to be involved. Measuring the impact of change can be seen by teachers as being very threatening, and it often alters the relationships between them and learners. It is therefore critically important that monitoring and evaluation are seen as a shared activity in which everyone learns how they can achieve better and more through the introduction of new technologies. It is often, for example, the case that pupils adapt to the use of new technologies more swiftly than teachers, and teachers need to be open to the possibility of learning new skills from their pupils.

The use of new technologies in learning has far more fundamental influences on people's lives than can be measured simply in terms of traditionally defined educational attainment targets. It is therefore difficult to design comprehensive 'measurement' procedures to evaluate the 'effectiveness' of such initiatives.

Moreover, even on the educational front, changes in performance levels in schools resulting from the use of ICTs might simply reflect the fact that pupils and teachers feel valued from the emphasis being placed on education through such programmes rather than any actual changes in the way that people learn. It is fundamentally important therefore both that managers identify exactly what it is that they want to measure in any such programme, and also that they are open to considering a far wider diversity of influences that they might envisage simply from an 'educational' perspective.

Different organisations adopt varied interpretations of 'capacity building', but ever since the Agenda 21 plan of action following the United Nations Conference on Environment and Development in 1992 the concept has gained increasing acceptance as being of fundamental importance to the delivery of 'development' objectives. Significantly, the Agenda 21 definition not only notes that 'capacity building encompasses the country's human, scientific, technological, organisational, institutional and resource capabilities', but also that one of its fundamental goals is 'to enhance the ability to evaluate and address the crucial questions related to policy choices and modes of implementation'.

At the heart of discussions about capacity building is therefore the notion of its role in measuring and evaluating. This theme has been central to the work of organisations such as the International Institute for Communication and Development in the Netherlands and the German Internationale Weiterbildung und Entwicklung GmbH, both of which have developed particular expertise at the interface between capacity building, ICT and evaluation.

All too often broad definitions of capacity building tend to get reduced in practice to mean enhancing the skills of a particular cadre of people, and in education systems this most usually means the teachers and administrators. However, if successful change management programmes involving new technologies are to be introduced, it is of critical importance that all of the key participants are involved.

One assumption behind the inclusion of such a wide range of stakeholders in the conceptualisation of monitoring and evaluation processes is that it takes the significance of education far beyond simply the school, college or university. It is about measuring the fundamental impacts of learning across many aspects of people's lives. For this to be effective, it is important that all those involved in monitoring and evaluation seek to adopt a collaborative attitude in developing shared expertise and understanding.

The introduction of ICTs into education is not a one-off process, but is instead the setting in motion of an entirely different modality of learning; one in which those involved seek to put in place a continued dynamic of enhancement. Striving for excellence, pushing the barriers back beyond traditionally accepted norms lies at the heart of what monitoring and evaluation is about. If we were not interested in enhancing learning, making it more readily available to people from different backgrounds and with a range of abilities and disabilities, there would be little point in seeking to measure the effects of changes in educational methods, systems and content.

All those involved in measuring these effects must therefore seek to work together supportively and creatively in designing systems that enable the lessons learnt to be introduced swiftly and efficiently back into the learning environment, so that good practices can be shared more widely and learners consequently benefit more effectively from the monitoring process. In effect, we need to create a virtuous cycle of learning enhancement, where everyone is able to benefit from being involved in the monitoring processes.

Professional Development and Training

One major limitation for change in ICT and education is that many of those involved in helping people to learn in both formal and non-formal contexts have little or no skills in the appropriate use of new technologies. This is particularly so in poorer countries, and most notably in

Africa. Furthermore, there have to date been rather few effective and sustainable schemes designed to enhance ICT4E literacy among teachers. To be sure, there are numerous projects that have sought to provide teachers with ICT skills, but many of these have been developed externally, often in the private sector, to develop skills that are relevant primarily in office environments. These are not necessarily those skills of most relevance in the classroom.

Knowing how a set of blended learning solutions, involving text, sound, imagery, touch and even taste and smell, can contribute to someone's learning is of much more value than simply giving teachers an ability to use word processing or database management skills! Tactile keyboards, for example, bring the Internet to life for blind people; audio cassettes transform learning for those who have difficulty seeing; the visual use of sign language opens up communication for the deaf and those with hearing disabilities.

There is, therefore, a profound need to develop systems and capacities that enable policy makers, administrators, teachers, and tutors to engage in professional staff training and development as an ongoing process within programmes and to link staff development more closely with service improvement and evaluation/ monitoring. Teachers and administrators must also have more opportunities to understand and learn from local problems and to invent local solutions. Increasing the proportion of well-trained ICT-literacy teachers and/or full-time ICT instructors is an essential element of enhanced human capacity development.

In recent years China has initiated several major ICT-supported programmes to enhance teacher training in its poorer Western provinces. These include the EU-China Gansu Basic Education Project, the UNDP and DFID supported programme in Gansu, Sichuan and Yunnan, and the Asian Development Bank's programme in Hunan. Monitoring and evaluation are key components of these initiatives.

In addition to service providers, there is also a need for the building of human capacity in the monitoring and evaluation sector. Many of those involved in monitoring and evaluation, particularly in poor countries, have little experience of such work, and it is crucial that simple but effective schemes are developed to enable them to contribute to, and benefit from, such activities.

The practical reality in most educational systems is that monitoring and evaluation, alongside measuring performance against targets, are frequently treated as separate and distinct activities, often undertaken by external reviewers or evaluators. In many African countries, where over 90% of Ministry of Education budgets are spent on teachers' salaries, governments and donors frequently see such external monitoring and evaluation as being less important than the actual delivery of education on the ground. This suggests that involving all participants in the education system in ongoing monitoring and evaluation as an integral part of their jobs would bring significant benefits. Much can be learnt from past experiences in incorporating effective monitoring and evaluation into ICT for education initiatives.

For example, management priorities were central to Singapore's Masterplan for IT in Education, with the intention being to use IT to 'promote greater efficiency in administration and communication, thereby supporting more effective educational management'. Moreover, one of the four key elements of the plan specifically addressed human resource development through training teachers in the purposeful use of IT in teaching, equipping them with core skills in teaching with IT, and involving partners from industry and institutions of higher learning in schools.

Between 1997 and 2000, most teachers in primary and secondary schools completed 8 to 10 core modules over 30 to 50 training hours, covering topics such as involving IT in pupil project work, appropriate teaching and learning strategies, and how to evaluate IT resources for their teaching. This programme was implemented through face-to-face workshops for core subjects, shared sessions for non-core subjects and dialogue sessions for the exchange of ideas and experiences amongst heads of departments. As a result, the MPITE evaluation report in 2001, suggested that 78% of teachers surveyed felt that the use of IT as a teaching tool had helped them to implement more learner-centred activities.

9

Online Higher Education

Online higher education provides different benefits and opportunities for students, higher education institutions, Governments and educational service providers. Each stakeholder has different needs and priorities. For example, established universities with high brand recognition are using online education to capitalise on their existing reputation and to èxpand enrolments. National Governments are funding new virtual universities through public/ private partnerships so as to find ways of expanding access to education without a significant rise in the education budget.

Not every stakeholder accepts the validity of all six drivers, neither from the economic nor from the educational point of view. For example, it can be argued that investing in online education may not be the best way of increasing either capacity or access and that traditional distance education may well cover this objective more effectively. Nevertheless, there are six main drives of online higher education. They are described below.

1. *To develop educational capacity*: The Internet makes it possible to reach more people over a wider area with limited access to traditional education in general or to specific higher education institutions. In this sense,

online higher education is an extension of the distance learning model. For example, the United Kingdom's Open University has long been providing distance education for UK and non-UK students, and it is now incorporating new technologies in the dissemination of education. The arrival of the Internet has brought additional access at a distance in the sense that most traditional and well-known universities did not engage in distance education, whereas they may do so now through online delivery. An example of a new institution that has been set up to increase capacity as a motive for investing in e-learning is the University of Pakistan, as explained in box 4.3.

2. *To improve the quality of learning*: There is a strong argument that the use of ICTs can increase the effectiveness and quality of learning by providing increased customisation, more flexibility and student choice. In the UNCTAD survey, the Virtual University of Monterrey emphasises the pedagogical benefits of e-learning: (a) it promotes the development of skills and attitudes, in addition to subject area knowledge; and (b) it offers students the possibility of extending their learning (via links, databases, etc.). However, teachers, students and employers have long contested the quality of online education, and there is a widespread perception that online degrees are of a poorer quality than those based on traditional study. In contrast, as part of a wider lobby promoting the values of ICTs and the Internet, there are groups, within both the educational and the IT community, that assert the value of e-learning in raising educational standards and effectiveness.

3. *To increase access (particularly for marginalised populations)*: E-learning can be used to provide

innovative solutions to address specific access issues that might make it difficult for potential students to participate in higher education. For example, the University of Palestine has attempted to use an element of online learning to enable students to interact with tutors when they are physically unable to reach the university because of roadblocks and other security measures in Gaza.

4. *To achieve cost-efficiencies*: The possibility of e-learning to expand capacity and access brings with it potential cost-efficiencies (reaching more students for less money) through reducing the cost per unit (or student) and therefore improving an institution's financial position. For many developed country institutions whose budgets have been reduced and which are facing increased domestic competition for funding, the potential to expand their market globally through virtual campuses and other e-learning ventures has been a strong driver. However, the argument that online education provides economies of scale, and thus cost-efficiencies, is contested. Depending on the infrastructure available, the initial start-up costs may be high and, if quality is to be maintained, the cost reduction per additional student numbers will be minimal. Thus, investing in online education solely for the sake of cost-efficiency is a high risk for any provider. In addition to economies of scale, the application of ICTs to education does provide other potential economic advantages: from the possibility of reselling educational content to third parties to opportunities to increase administrative efficiency, and from better student management systems and access to better information for decision-making to improved communications.

5. *To enhance the uptake of ICT skills and infrastructure, so as to promote a knowledge economy*: Perhaps the key driver for online education at the macro-policy level is that it will enhance ICT skills and infrastructure, and thus serve to reinforce the promotion of a "knowledge economy". Developing an e-learning strategy can complement other national ICT policies. Indeed, there are synergies between different sectors. For example, in the United Kingdom, the Department of Trade and Industry has targeted educational and training services—in particular online education—as a key area for overseas export. The export potential of UK education is underpinned by national investment by the Department for Education and Skills in creating a market for online material through measures such as e-learning credits. One of the potential benefits for Governments in adopting an e-learning strategy is that it can promote the use of ICTs and contribute to the development and use of ICT infrastructure (universities are early adapters of ICTs). Moreover, it can provide a market for related industries, including software, content development, media and other educational services.

6. *Because it's there: survival and marketing strategy*: There is also the perception that e-learning is worth investing in because, to some degree, it represents "the future" and if some institutions have e-learning capacity, then other universities need to invest in order to be able to compete. For example, in response to the question about motivation for e-learning the University of Jzvaskyla, Finland, replied "necessity...because of European development and Bologna processes in higher education". Similarly, Monterrey University makes a selling point of using the most up-to-date

technologies available: "uses the most advanced technological, multimedia, and audiovisual resources for instruction".

In today's globalised information society, falling behind in access to and use of ICTs (often referred to as the digital divide) can lead to lost economic and development opportunities, and can exacerbate existing inequalities between and within countries. To overcome this digital divide, it is necessary to develop ICT infrastructure and skills as well as an understanding of the appropriate use and application of ICTs relevant to different needs and contexts. However, unless underserved populations are consciously and proactively targeted, any national digital divide will increase.

Using online education to bridge the digital divide is an attractive proposition, but it will only happen if a coherent inclusive strategy is put in place together with the necessary resources. Partnerships with private enterprises can partially alleviate resources restraints. Currently, international donors, private enterprises and other players have a strong interest in investing in online education. In the information society, information obviously has essential value. Economies are increasingly dependent on both the information that is available to them and the resources with which to use it. But for this information to be valuable, it has to be relevant to the user, and to the latter's context and purpose. This applies to every user, from the savvy IT student to the basic reader, for every context, from the international market to a small rural community, and for every use and sector from services to agriculture.

One of the concerns about the proliferation of online education is the dominance of developed countries in producing and disseminating content and information: most

Internet content is in English and originates in developed countries. The effects can already be seen: citizens are unable to access relevant information because it is in a language they do not understand, is irrelevant to their context and incompatible with their existing level of technology and skills. Given that professional content is largely created and shared through universities, online higher education offers an opportunity for national Governments interested in devoting efforts and resources to the creation, promotion and use of local content. New initiatives such as open content and open source are putting in place some of the necessary frameworks for the open snaring of information.

Online Higher Education Market

Online higher education is a potentially profitable global market. The OECD predicted in 2001 that there will be 30-80 million online students in the world by 2025. The online higher education market is composed of goods and services that include software applications that enable interaction via the Internet, course content, support services (such as accreditation or education management) and the actual dissemination of education. In addition, online higher education requires products not restricted to the specific online higher education market, such as ICT infrastructure.

With online education new stakeholders have entered the higher education market, and the bargaining power of existing stakeholders has changed. Potentially, teachers are losing influence to software developers who create structures and systems for teachers to fit their content into. Some students can have increased power because they can now choose among different educational providers, even without leaving home. Any projection about the size of the online market has to be treated with caution since only a limited number of official statistics include specific indicators on the use of online education and there are not yet internationally comparable indicators.

Most indicators related to ICTs and education have been produced for e-learning in general, for primary and secondary education or for the corporate market, and this leaves a large information gap in online higher education. Thus, current estimates on the impact of online higher education are based on these other variables or on the impact of the distance education market. The Economist Intelligence Unit ranking grades 60 countries according to their e-learning readiness. In other words, it ranks countries on their ability to produce, use and expand Internetbased learning—both informal and formal, at work and at school, in government and throughout society. This ranking assesses e-learning on the basis of four categories: education, industry, government and society.

Within each category the assessment is based on four factors that make e-learning possible: connectivity—"the quality and extent of Internet infrastructure"; capability—"a country's ability to deliver and consume e-learning, based on literacy rates, and trends in training and education"; content—"the quality and pervasiveness of online learning materials" and culture—"behaviours, beliefs and institutions that support e-learning". Although the ranking examines a broader sector than higher education, it does provide some kind of map of the state of e-learning internationally. Among the leaders are the Nordic countries, the United States and Canada, the United Kingdom, Switzerland, Australia and East Asian tigers. All these countries are recognised as having strong educational systems and high levels of ICT penetration, as well as a competitive market. They are then followed by other European countries and other Asian countries.

In the middle ranking there are some of the most developed Eastern European countries, as well as the most developed Latin American nations. These countries have in general benefited from government policies and from a commitment to exploring different ways of funding ICT investment. Counter-intuitively, given their strong investment in ICTs, South Africa only ranks 40th, and surprisingly India and China, despite their large distance education markets, are towards the bottom of the rankings. Given the limitations of the data presented we can judge that India's high score in the industry category is brought down by low scores in the other categories, while China's score is particularly low in the education category. According to IDC analysts, the corporate e-learning market was valued at $6.6 billion in 2002, of which $5.2 billion was in the United States. This figure is expected to rise to $23.7 billion in 2006.

The expansion of e-learning in corporate organisations benefits from, among other things, having available ICT infrastructure, having resources for training, and in the case of international dissemination of e-learning the opportunity to save on travel costs. Much of the literature agrees that for a wide range of policy reasons, such as equality motivations or ability to raise funds, financial returns in higher education are not as secure as they are in the corporate e-learning market. Thus we can expect the size of the online higher education market to be smaller. From this analysis, it is clear that the United States is the market leader in the use and export of online higher education. With an estimated 80 per cent share of the corporate e-learning sector, it is expected to have a high market share in the online higher education market.

The Sloan Consortium estimates that in the autumn of 2002 over 1.6 million students in the United States took at least one online course, which represents 11 per cent of all US students. Over one third of those students (578,000) took all their courses online. Moreover, Worldwidelearncites a report by Capella University estimating that "distance learning is expected to increase in the US by 900 percent to include 750,000 students fully online by 2005". Japan's Ministry of Public Management puts the value of Japan's e-learning revenues in 2003 at $770 million. According to NetLearning, the Japanese e-learning market is a small proportion of that in the United States, only one thirtieth. In particular, the value of the corporate e-learning market was $290 million in 2003. This is a great difference, even when the fact that Japanese GDP is only half of United States GDP is taken into account.

In Canada there is a strong higher education market both for English-speaking and for Frenchspeaking students, and Canadian education has a good international reputation. Athabasca University, which is regarded as the Canadian Open University, claims to be the first to offer an online MBA and currently hosts over 30,000 students.

In Australia all universities are engaged in online education to some extent, and 207 courses are fully online. Australia is a regional leader for higher education, able to attract Asian students looking for education in English close to home. For example, Australia increased the share of international students studying in Australian post secondary institutions through distance learning and offshore programmes from 18 per cent to 35 per cent between 1997 and 2001.

The United Kingdom has a long tradition of distance education, for example the Open University, and is further promoting e-learning and online education in its national and international market. Despite the uncertainty surrounding the UK eUniversity programme, a government-backed initiative to market online courses of UK universities abroad, other universities are investing heavily in international online education. For example, the University of Liverpool has signed a 10-year agreement with Sylvan Learning Systems to provide its courses online. In Eastern Europe, online education is patchy.

The good higher education infrastructure is not always matched by extensive access to and use of ICT. Nevertheless the newcomers in the European Union expect that accession will help minimise major obstacles such as expensive ICT hardware and the scarcity of quality content, limited digital literacy and language skills. Know-how for the future includes experience in government public-private initiatives in e-learning as well as international collaboration at the higher education level. For example, Hungary has one degree—in law—offered fully through the Internet, by the Pázamány Péter Catholic University, and the Government of Hungary is proposing a searchable database of learning material.

In Latin America and the Caribbean, the Monterrey Virtual University has been able to establish itself as a market leader. Countries such as Argentina, Chile and Brazil are popular destinations for private e-learning enterprises. There are already a number of online courses from US providers such as the University of Phoenix, UNext and the Monterrey Virtual University, as well as a limited number of traditional universities offering online courses.

An example of the latter is the Universidad Virtual de Quilmes in Argentina, which in collaboration with the Universtitat Oberta de Catalunya in Barcelona, has launched a private virtual university. In Peru, the Inter-American Development Bank backed the Instituto Tecnológico Superior, a private business and technology school, to develop virtual professional training programmes. These are not formal higher education courses, but seven-week courses. Their success confirms that with the necessary backing, online education can be successful in attracting students. But countries that are less developed are finding it difficult to benefit from e-learning and even less from online education. The example of Bolivia provides a useful corrective to some of the claims about higher education by illustrating many of the challenges that some countries face regarding online education.

In Asia, online education is growing in the richer and more technically advanced developing countries. For example, in Malaysia there are two institutions playing a leading role in the regional online higher education market: UNITAR, a private virtual university offering 20 academic programmes in the field of business, IT and social sciences to more than 8,000 students at 11 study centres in Malaysia, Cambodia and Thailand, and MUST, the Malaysia University of Science and Technology, a private research institution set up in collaboration with the Massachusetts Institute of Technology. In contrast, India and China have a long tradition of open and distance education, with experience in the application of technologies to education, such as satellite and radio, but for the moment online higher education is only starting to be developed.

In Africa there is the African Virtual University, originally created by the World Bank and now a donor-led and mixed distance/e-learning initiative. For French-speaking countries there is a specific initiative funded by the Francophonie: the Campus Numérique Francophone, which establishes ICT-equipped centres to promote the use of online learning in universities in French-speaking West Africa. Additionally, there are a multitude of donor-led educational projects, focused on bringing new technologies into African education, such as teacher training in South Africa. However, the adoption of online education has not been entirely successful.

Dramatic failures have already been hitting the headlines: Hawkridge cites, among others, Fathom ($40 million), a Columbia University initiative; New York Online ($20 million) from New York University; Temple University, which shut down its business without offering a single course; and the UK Open University initiative to establish itself in the United States (£9 million). Additionally, the latest disappointment in online international higher education has been the UK eUniversity. The reasons for these failures are varied, including problems of accreditation, lack of transparent governance and above all the failure to sell the product and attract enough students. These examples prove that the availability of funding and resources does not guarantee the sustainability of a project.

Most developing countries are progressively introducing ICT into their education systems subject to the availability of Internet infrastructure and ICT skills. The use of the Internet for higher education is still very limited, but technology in general has long been used to provide education, both through computers in schools and through distance education. The difference between offering one course online and a full degree online is also becoming more relevant for students. Universities that want to be able to reach students at a distance are making every effort to deliver full degrees online or to promote recognition of their individual courses so that the courses can count towards degrees of other universities. Online higher education in many cases evolves from distance education.

Open universities, such as in India and the United Kingdom, have long been using technology in a number of ways to deliver courses at a distance. The transformation from distance to online education is a more natural evolution: instructors are familiar with teaching at a distance, the university already has a structure to develop course materials, and students are used to interacting with teachers and one another across space and time. In marketing terms, online delivery has given more credibility to distance education, which has often been seen as second best to traditional, face-to-face higher education. It seems that Governments are more inclined to provide funding for online projects than to fund distance education.

For example, according to Tu and Twu, in Taiwan Province of China the Government was assigning between $3,125 and $9,375 for a traditional university student, while the expenditure for a distance education student is $625. One of the trends we have seen in higher education is the growth of private providers and an increasingly blurred division between private and public provision. In the United States, with its particular pattern of private higher education, only 4 to 5 per cent of all students are enrolled with for-profit providers. However, 33 per cent of all online students are enrolled with the same provider. It would seem that private for-profit interests are leading in providing online educational services.

Additionally, several public institutions are providing online education through a for-profit institution, such as the failed New York University Online initiative. As in offline education, alliances between for-profit and not-for-profit organisations, and between private and public institutions, provide strategic benefits but also carry governance and sustainability risks, as well as access, equality, quality and ownership implications.

Influence of Internet on the International Trade in Higher Education

The opening of trade in educational services is surrounded by uncertainty and current data are insufficient to provide an accurate picture of the value of international trade in online educational services. Nevertheless, some hypotheses about the impact of the Internet on the international trade in higher education can be formulated. The Internet is promoting international trade in higher education services by facilitating the dissemination of educational content and services through online distribution. Paulsen indicates that there are 200,000 courses available on the Internet. Whether this is an exaggeration or reality, it gives a flavour of the enormous variety of online educational supply.

Online education is also promoting trade in other modes of supplying higher educational services, such as the movement of students and commercial presence. Online educational providers generally need to work with, or are requested to set up, a local subsidiary to better support students and market their programmes as well as for assessment purposes. Moreover, blended learning is in many cases becoming a preferred mode for engaging in education. Online education offers an additional mode of entry to educational institutions that want to provide their services in countries with protective educational markets.

It should be noted in this regard that developed countries are the major exporters of online higher education services, and developing nations are the net importers of such services. Given that few countries have regulations covering the provision of online services by foreign entities, online education can be a more attractive option for foreign suppliers to offer higher education services in a given country. If national Governments limit the establishment of commercial education providers, the Internet makes it possible to circumvent regulatory barriers. Online education is becoming an option for students who have difficulties in travelling abroad, and this is particularly relevant for citizens from developing countries.

Multiple forces are shaping the direction and numbers of students crossing borders. In general, more restrictive entry regulations for students favour online education or other international and regional markets. The passage of the US Patriot Act has been linked to a decrease of up to 30 per cent in the number of international students enrolled in US colleges and universities. This could promote other destinations, such as Australia or the United Kingdom, and online education. But travel restrictions can also jeopardise online education.

A large number of online courses still require attendance at short workshops, and visa regulations tend to discriminate against online students. The application of ICTs to education is allowing for the unbundling of academic functions, which in turn promotes international trade in educational services by fostering specialisation and customisation of educational services. The unbundling of academic functions occurs when multiple players intervene in the education supply chain: one party may create the course content, another delivers it, a third institution manages the resources, another provides the accreditation, and so on. The drawback to the unbundling of academic functions is that it challenges ownership and control of the educational service, and can consequently jeopardise its quality.

The Internet is also increasing trade in higher education services by facilitating the reuse and reselling of higher education resources to serve the lifelong learning needs of the information society. In a rapidly changing, technology-dependent economy, lifelong learning has become increasingly important for ensuring the necessary and continuous updating of skills. As a consequence, the rise of lifelong learning is accelerating the convergence of different educational sectors, including corporate training, higher education and the "other" key sector in international education (language training). As the Internet is already widely used in the corporate training sector, one might expect its use in higher education to further facilitate the reuse and trade of educational services from one sector to another.

Investments in Online Higher Education

As with any public investment in ICTs the most substantial objections to online education arise from the opportunity cost of investing in ICTs and not in other programmes judged to be more vital. Four criteria help determine financial decisions for any investment, including online higher education: profitability, affordability, sustainability and efficiency. The most common question regarding the profitability of online education is whether it is cheaper than traditional education. A starting point for answering this question is to examine the cost structure of e-learning courses.

Traditionally, studies scrutinising the comparative value of different educational models focused on a cost accountancy exercise. Such studies were primarily concerned with comparing the unitary cost per student or per course. However, as described above, there are a variety of online education models. Therefore, unless applied to a specific case, any cost structure analysis can only serve as guidance. Additionally, this type of analysis is particularly difficult in the field of education, where educational institutions tend to have ill-defined cost centres. The general economic argument for online education is based on economies of scale.

Online education is potentially cheaper than face-to-face education when a large number of students are targeted. Theoretically, the additional cost per student is limited, and therefore a large customer base allows the recovery of the significant investments made on infrastructure and on product development. For example, the Monterrey Virtual University claims that online courses are cheaper than face-to-face courses. However, the economies-of-scale argument has yet to be proved. Some large-scale e-learning programmes have failed despite their aim of reaching more customers. For example, the UK eUniversity project, which has cost £62 million (approximately $114 million), aimed at jointly marketing UK online courses abroad but only managed to recruit 900 students (instead of the 5,000 targeted) in its first year of operation.

Secondly, the economic rationale for some online educational projects, in particular those on the model of "independent online courses", is not based on economies of scale but on providing valuable knowledge in a specific field and on being financed by donors and/or users. For example, UNCTAD's Train For Trade programme depends on donor funding, the content is developed in-house, and competition is limited to the search for donor monies. The content is highly specialised, and based on the core of the organisation's knowledge. While it provides opportunities for the dissemination of knowledge, concerns about self-sustainability, particularly in an increasingly competitive environment, and because of the limits to funding (for example, if the e-learning fashion were to pass), should be addressed.

Thirdly, experience shows that currently a large number of projects have still not gone beyond (or have failed before finishing) the pilot phase, and thus it is difficult to judge where full-size projects could be successful.

Finally, quality and customisation raise doubts about any possible economies of scale for online higher education. Maintaining an acceptable tutor/student ratio cannot be achieved cheaply without alienating teachers, and customisation to local culture involves a high degree of content and pedagogical expertise that requires a significant proportion of any budget.

However, there is a broader question regarding the importance of cost: does it really matter if online education is cheaper than traditional education? From the individual point of view students will be assessing whether their efforts will be remunerated in terms of increased life opportunities, private institutions may look at further utilising existing infrastructure, increasing loyalty and improving the quality of their services, and educational policy makers will be seeking to increase access and further ICT skills.

Without doubt some institutions in developed countries are enjoying returns on their investment in online education, but the potential for developing countries may be more constrained. For example, online provision increases international competition for students, which in turn has an impact on the ability of institutions in developing countries charging higher prices to non-resident students, given their low brand recognition or their catchment area.

Affordability, or the question of whether Governments, institutions and students can afford online education is a related issue that can be overlooked in the profitability criteria. Is the Government's educational budget able to afford the provision of online education? Would lower-income students be able to access online higher education? It can be argued that national Governments' investment in online higher education is justified when it allows the participation of students from lower-income levels.

Online education tends to be associated with private provision, particularly in higher education. In some cases, such as MUST, the online project has only gone ahead when the national Government has been able to confirm funding for all national students participating in the programme. It seems that much of the boom in ICTs in education is being promoted by developed economies and that international funding provides a strong driving force. However, the capacity of international funding to finance higher education is rather limited, in terms of both time and the proportion of overall spending. Thus national Governments are entrusted with the responsibility of taking crucial financing decisions for higher education, by investing themselves and/or encouraging the private sector to invest.

The third major criterion is the economic sustainability of any online education programme. Governments of developed countries and international organisations, including the World Bank and the United Nations, have been actively involved in promoting new online higher education initiatives. The question arises as to what will happen at the end of the programme when the specific funds earmarked for online education have been used and the programme is handed to the local institution, and/or when the funding priorities and private investment interest shift to other areas.

ICTs increase specialisation, which in turn can bring more efficiency to the educational sector by enhancing internal organisation, communication and knowledge sharing, and by allowing teachers to specialise in their field of expertise. The Internet is also allowing the unbundling of academic functions and thus specialisation, as well as promoting the convergence of different educational sectors, by facilitating the reuse of educational content. This can yield new efficiencies and markets, and allow for local customisation. However, unbundling can also bring with it possible loss of ownership of educational resources and processes. Additionally, the efficiency of online education needs to be measured against educational objectives and context.

It is clear that what is efficient in a developed economy, with an already established ICT coverage, may not be so efficient for a low-income economy where the number of people with access to the Internet is much smaller. To summarise: traditionally, the financial analysis of higher education has focused on two areas—firstly, comparing the cost of producing a course or educating a student, and secondly on analysing individual initiatives and their profitability. Both areas of analysis cast doubts on the profitability of online learning, and although there are potential earnings with economies of scale and individual financial success stories, there have already been many failures and there may be more when donors withdraw their funds. Analysis of the three other criteria—affordability, sustainability and efficiency—are also necessary in order to evaluate the economic viability of online higher education, and in particular to enable national Governments to take sound decisions.

ICT Infrastructure

Technology is not neutral, neither economically nor pedagogically. From an economics perspective, the use (or lack of use) of different technologies has a variable impact on access, cost, efficiency and ownership. What follows is a brief presentation of different online education technologies and their markets, as well as an analysis of their impact. The description given recognises infrastructural issues and focuses on the most recent debates on ICT applications for online education. The use and the adoption of online higher education require ICT infrastructure. To maximise the use of ICTs in education computers and software are indispensable, and in the particular case of online learning access to the Internet is also a prerequisite.

Reliable and fast connectivity, as well as sufficient bandwidth, are of particular importance in order to make full use of the range of e-learning software and applications—from animated simulations used to enhance learning in engineering or medicine to video conferencing for increased interactivity between students and teachers at a distance. The ability of a region, State or nation to develop e-learning depends on the existence of a strong ICT infrastructure. For example, the Survey of e-Learning Readiness prepared by the Economist Intelligence Unit's (EIU), when compared with the EIU's broader e-Readiness Survey, shows a strong correlation between e-learning readiness and general ICT readiness. However, as the outliers in the EIU's survey illustrates, connectivity is just one part of the picture.

The building of knowledge economies and of the related human-resource capacity also requires the availability of non-electronic information and knowledge sources (e.g. libraries, books and journals available to the public), competent educational management, a culture of change and sufficient educational funds. A corollary then is that if online education is to be successful, funding of ICT infrastructure should not be at the expense of other knowledge resources. For stakeholders producing or providing education in developing nations the question is how best to maximise the potential of online education and the technological infrastructure available to achieve their objectives.

Some providers or Governments believe that the only way forward is to increase connectivity or improve access to new technology. However, others, particularly local developers and providers, defend the use of low or intermediate technology or concentrating access provision in community or distance learning centres, such as the ones used by Indira Gandhi Open University.

ICT Applications

The Internet has had a major impact on education in terms of both content creation and distribution. Digital technology has facilitated the creation and distribution of content, but the Internet is also allowing wider access to these tools so as to create and share knowledge through global resource exchange and instant/distant content discussion. What follows is an examination of the structures and products that support online content creation, delivery and management. Designers and teachers use a wide variety of tools to create content, such as word processors, presentation software, audio, video and animation. They also use ICT tools to evaluate students (e.g. assessment tools).

Moreover, they use ICT-based communication to enhance teacher-student or student interaction. Traditional methods, such as audiocassettes and videocassettes, are and will continue to be widely used in developing countries, for example by the Indira Gandhi University in India, and even in online courses provided by Western institutions (e.g. the UK Open University). To state the obvious: the creation and delivery of content requires course management, and vice versa, and both are reliant on the infrastructure available. For example, distributing content through videoconference will only be possible if the intended audience has access to videoconferencing equipment as well as the knowledge and motivation to use it.

Educational materials for online education are normally referred to as courseware, and learning objects are the modular units of instruction that can be stored and searched through databases and networks, used and reused, aggregated or re-engineered to suit the purposes of multiple institutions, faculty members or instructional developers. These courseware systems are at the core of online education. Producing such systems is expensive, but their value is maximised if they are designed to be flexible, customisable, interoperable, easy to update and reused.

Online education should be more than simply the posting of educational information online. It is the provision via the Internet of fully realised courses, with curriculum, bibliography, pedagogical sequence and so on. The large majority of online courses are developed in the fields of business management and ICT related areas. These are popular areas in traditional higher education, but additionally, they have proved good for online learning because they can be standardised and generally require less face-to-face interaction or practice outside the computer. However, other subjects such as education and primary health care studies, which would normally require a strong face-to-face/practical experience, are also popular online courses.

Suppliers of online education primarily focus on courses that can be easily produced and reproduced, but also on where there is a large demand. Internet delivery is particularly popular with postgraduate courses, presumably because of their shorter duration and greater independence, as well as their popularity with full-time professionals. A survey of online education and services in Australia shows that the courses most repeated are those leading to ecommerce and online education diplomas—that is, the object, as well as the means of study, is the Internet—and that 90 percent of the online courses at universities are at postgraduate level.

But as we have seen with the different models of online higher education, other business models are used in distributing online specialised content since this specialisation is the core and strength of the providing institution. One such example would be the Master's programme in Leadership for Sustainable Development delivered by LEAD, and accredited by Middlesex University in the United Kingdom. The programme, funded by private donors, supports a limited number of international students to become leaders and maintains a network for sustainable development.

The growth of the Internet has led to increased availability of content and, as with public libraries, there is a demand for knowledge to be shared and freely or cheaply accessible. A well-known initiative to make courses publicly available online is Open Courseware. A renowned example is the Massachussetts Institute of Technology (MIT) OpenCourseWare (OCW) initiative, which makes selected MIT courses online available for free Posting information online is not the same as providing an online course.

In some cases, all that is posted on the OCW site is the syllabus and bibliography. Whether because of intellectual property rights restrictions or management motivations, OCW does not offer access to lectures, explanations and discussions or to the key readings. For most users the OCW initiative is not sufficient, particularly for those in developing countries where access to reading material is limited. An additional obstacle is that all information is in English and OCW's plans are that it will continue this way.

Higher education institutions from developing countries are greatly interested in pursuing an open courseware initiative, but not at any price. They have cultural and language concerns as well as the more general infrastructure concern, and they recognise current intellectual property rights barriers. The interest lies in accessing information but also making accessible information from their own countries and communities. Currently, there are informal knowledge sharing initiatives targeting the needs of developing nations, such as the international Open Knowledge Network consortium, but not at the specific level of higher education. Professionals from developed and developing countries have suggested that open courseware, should:

1. Provide educational resources for college and university faculties to adapt them in accordance with their curricular and pedagogical needs;
2. Include the technology to support open, meaningful access and use of courseware;
3. Include at a minimum the course description, syllabus, calendar and at least one of the following: lecture notes, demonstrations, simulations, illustrations or learning objects.

The Internet is also having a major impact on research and publication. It has led to information being available to more people, new publication opportunities, networking being enhanced through newsgroups and other mechanisms for collaborating across borders. For most scholars in developed countries it is almost unimaginable to engage in research without access to the Internet. The Web has produced a huge increase in "grey literature"—online publication of research outside the traditional mechanisms of academic publishing. The opening up of knowledge through online databases and journals has had a transforming effect. However, access to a large number of established refereed journals and databases is still controlled through subscription, and the ownership of the intellectual property contained in journals is tightly controlled by publishers.

Secondly, the Internet is challenging and transforming academic research and publishing by establishing new models of peer review and publishing which will influence the balance of power as regards who owns intellectual assets. This shift has the potential to democratise not just access to knowledge but also ownership and control over how that knowledge is used, with clear benefits and advantages for institutions in developing countries.

Additionally, the separation between production and distribution, as in traditional higher education, is blurred. In some cases online content is developed by the provider, the teacher himself/ herself or the university (e.g. LEAD develops its own high-quality content), while at other times external content is used, adapted or not.

Content Management

Content is provided primarily through Learning Management Systems (LMS). The newer and more advanced version (Learning Content Management Systems) offers additional features that focus on content management and authoring. LMS integrate the management of content—online modules and communication tools—with student registration and administration procedures. They enable an institution to develop electronic learning materials, to offer these courses electronically, and then to use the same system to test and evaluate the students and to generate student databases in which individual results and progress can be charted.

Universities use commercial and in-house learning management systems to manage their online programmes. The market for LMS is estimated at around $500 million (table 1). There are two major international players: WebCT (United States), a privately held company, created in 1995 with $125 million secured through six rounds of equity financing, which has a 33.5 per cent market share in the United States; and Blackboard (United States), which had a total revenue of $92.5 million in 2003, has 5.3 million active users at more than 1,600 institutions in more than 70 countries and has a 42.5 per cent market share in the United States, covering all educational sectors. The LMS market is still at an early stage of development.

Table 1: Learning management systems market (millions of dollars)

Estimation by:	2001	2003	2004	2006
IDC	$ 800			$3600
Simba Information	$ 200			
Lifelong Learning Report			$ 529	
Bersin & Associates		$ 350		

With over 140 commercial offerings worldwide the market is highly competitive with few leaders, mainly based in the United States, but with low market share. For example, Bersin maintains that the market share of the largest player is no more than 7 per cent of the market. A European study found as many as 52 different commercial and 35 self-developed LMS in 113 educational institutions. Moreover, institutions do not seem to be especially loyal to a particular brand, switching between different packages or using several systems in one university. For example, a survey of Australian universities found that out of 40 respondents, 29 used WebCT, 20 had their own in-house system and 17 were using Blackboard.

The LMS market will be expanding (with new and updated products, and a diversified language offer) and is expected to undergo some consolidation through the merger of providers. The provision of more languages and features, together with increased standardisation or open source systems development, will reduce institutions' incentive to develop their own software. However, economic rationale does not always play a part in opting for the in-house development of a system; rather, decisions are often driven by the bargaining power and interests of ICT departments.

Evidence from a study of LMS systems in European institutions suggests that IT sections of universities and other institutions attach great importance to developing their own platform and not buying programmes developed by others. For example, in the United States only 7.2 per cent of institutions have developed their own LMS, whereas in Europe 35 out of 113 (32 per cent) have developed their own system. Universities have developed and/or acquired their own LMS, benefiting from available free and open source systems or from partnerships with other institutions.

ICTs have allowed the production and distribution of content in a variety of electronic formats incorporating different media. The ability to use content on different platforms is an asset, particularly in education, where the potential for content exchange is unlimited. Currently, there are two complementary approaches to ensure interoperability and transferability: free and open source software, and open standards. Although their approaches differ, international initiatives such as SCORM and the OKI are playing a central role in promoting openness and reusability of content. Free and open-source software (FOSS) is software that has made its source code public, and allows users to modify the programme and thus customise and adapt it to particular needs.

FOSS, already widely used for web server technology, has a more limited presence in desktop software. However, in the field of education, it has the potential to become widely used in management systems and on desktops.

Firstly, universities are at the centre of open software development that is, there is a strong connection between users and developers, which facilitates the continuous updating and support that ICT software requires. The list of current open source course management software shows how most software is developed in or with the support of a university.

Secondly, the positive externalities of education provide a strong incentive for sharing and maximising the use of existing technology and content.

Thirdly, FOSS, at least until there is a full commitment to interoperability, can provide the necessary communication links between different IT platforms and tools.

Finally, the education software sector is still in its infancy and neither the commercial nor the FOSS market has a monopoly; consequently, early developers have the opportunity to find a niche.

One FOSS example is the Open Knowledge Initiative (OKI) course-management system. This developed from collaboration among top US and UK universities. Led in the United States by MIT, and supported by a philanthropic donation, the OKI is a scalable and sustainable reference platform designed for Internet-enabled education, which specifically addresses the needs of higher education. As its web page notes, where possible it uses open standards and its code is available to everybody, including commercial vendors.

A study of 117 institutions involved in e-learning (87 in the United States and 30 elsewhere) showed that when institutions bought new e-learning products, in 16 per cent of cases they would choose free and open source, while 80 per cent would choose commercial products, and only 4 per cent would choose in-house development.

The second approach to ensure interoperability is the commitment to and use of open standards both by commercial and by open-source packages. Open standards are transparent descriptions of data and behaviour that form the basis of interoperability. They are crucial for maximising the use and reuse of different media and content, and they guarantee interoperability, which open source software per se does not. However, in practice, developers and providers show different levels of commitment to open standards. Because they wish to protect their product or to reduce software development time, standardisation is not always regarded as suitable.

An example of an open standard that has achieved some success in corporate learning programmes in the United States is the Sharable Courseware Object Reference Model (SCORM) initiative. This initiative, which began in 1997, is part of a wider US government programme for distributing learning. Its aim is to foster the creation of reusable learning content. The initiative has identified critical technical interface points around which standards for web-based learning technologies might be developed. The first version was released on 31 January, 2000, and since then 64 LMS have adopted SCORM standards. It should be noted that the ability to use content on different platforms and to connect different systems provides further efficiencies.

In terms of ICT efficiency the optimum choice to promote interoperability is a combination of open source and open systems. Some institutions have already paid a high price in entering into contracts with fixed technology systems, and those that have to take decisions in the future will benefit from analysing the potential costs of all the options available.

Legal Issues

Access to, and cost, ownership and efficiency of, online education are conditioned by technology, but also by the broader policy context and particularly the existing legal framework and the general level of ICT skills. The legal framework affecting online higher education extends from specific regulations in the field of education to broader legal issues, including intellectual property rights, commercial law, security and authentication, electronic payment systems, consumer protection, applicable law, and fiscal and customs regulations.

Both sets of regulations shape the ability to buy, sell, develop and use online higher education. For example, in order to sell a degree online an institution needs to be accredited and, the degree needs to be recognised; students want to be protected against provision default and unauthorised use of their personal data, course developers want to control the use of their work and Governments want to control the quality of online educational programmes.

Various legal issues are affecting the online higher education. Most important of them are: accreditation and recognition, and intellectual property rights (IPRs). These issues are of special interest to developing countries since these are the countries that suffer most from lack of access to, and recognition of, their knowledge resources, and are the net importers of online higher education.

Accreditation

Accreditation is the currency of higher education. While learning for its own sake has cultural value and in some circumstances can be viewed as a leisure activity, in economic terms it is accredited and certified qualifications that count. Through appropriate quality assurance approaches and accreditation systems, Governments and accredited institutions ensure and promote quality in higher education, support the transferability of degrees across states, regions or nations and guarantee the authenticity of a degree.

National quality assurance and accreditation systems vary from one country to another and in many developing countries are non-existent. The lack of trust in a national accreditation system seriously undermines its educational credibility both nationally and internationally. Each government has its own policies to provide accreditation; for example, in the United States accreditation is provided through independent not-for-profit organisations, and the only role of the US Department of Education is to oversee such accreditation institutions, not the actual educational institutions themselves. This high degree of institutional autonomy contrasts with European education systems, where autonomy to borrow money, to invest in new products and, therefore, to market degrees online and internationally is more limited.

As regards accreditation, online higher education is an issue in the key areas of quality, transferability, authenticity and branding. The growth of harder-to-regulate online higher education, as well as the increase in the number of higher education students, and the internationalisation and privatisation of education, provides challenges for national accreditation systems. Online education increases the number of programmes and individual modules, as well as the number of institutions offering educational services. This creates problems of evaluation, inspection and examination, and educational services providers may find it easier to circumvent local regulation by going online.

Quality assurance and accreditation systems tend to be weak in most developing countries, particularly in Africa and the Arab regions. However, in the light of increasing demand for and supply of higher education, accreditation systems are being revised in those regions. Countries such as Malaysia and South Africa are already working on updating their quality assurance and accreditation systems. For example, South Africa established a Higher Education Quality Committee in May 2001 to tackle the large number of private institutions offering higher education programmes illegally. Despite the current initiatives to update national accreditation systems, they tend to ignore the specific features of online education, leaving this mode of delivery in a limbo.

But there are some innovative examples: in India the National Assessment and Accreditation Council has now been asked to prepare for the responsibility of accrediting the international educational offerings in all forms, including electronically. The existence of national systems of accreditation means that institutions recognised in one country are not automatically recognised in another. For example, the UK Open University has failed to gain accreditation in the United States. Online higher education circumvents this obstacle: it allows institutions recognised in one country to provide online education in another country without needing a specific accreditation since the qualification on offer will be accredited in the exporting country.

In online education what counts is the ability for a nation and/or institution to develop a reputable and desirable brand for its online courses. However, in some cases accreditation systems aiming to ensure quality make requirements that can hamper the flexibility of online higher education internationally. Examples include making it compulsory to have a national licence to work or for students to engage in some element of face-to-face contact so as to minimise the risk of cheating, or even requiring the same curriculum as the home-campus version. All these are part of the Malaysian quality assurance framework. Renowned university brands sell well offline and provide a valuable asset for their online endeavours.

Additionally, other universities have successfully built their brand and recognition solely online. Students look for recognition, either through brand value or accreditation of their studies by developed country institutions or developing country regional leaders. Developing countries in particular suffer from poor recognition of their degrees, and the arrival of online education is a further threat. Before the advent of the Internet, poor institutions sought partnerships with counterparts in richer countries that could provide them with the established brand recognition. With online courses, students who have the requisite resources can increasingly study in prestigious universities while staying at home and opt for the more internationally valuable foreign degrees.

Role of Intellectual Property Rights (IPR)

IPRs play a role in determining the ability to access, produce, copy and distribute content and specific expressions of knowledge. Having access to knowledge does not prevent others from benefiting from such knowledge. However, economic policy has long supported the need to grant temporary property rights to innovators so as to enable a return on their investments and thus encourage them to continue innovating, thereby contributing to a society in general. On the other hand, IPRs also act as a deterrent to innovation by limiting free access to knowledge and information.

The effects are notably greater for developing countries that lack resources to pay for access, and that are net importers of such goods and services. Since education is a public good, and is strongly based on knowledge, the application of IPRs to education is of particular importance. The arrival of the Internet has aggravated the conflict in several ways. The Internet is promoting more knowledge exchange around the world—from developed to developing countries, and vice versa. Since online education services derive from diverse sources (music, software, content, design, media, etc.) they are also restricted by varied protecting rights, which are now enforced by both technical and legal methods.

Moreover, free public access to knowledge (e.g. through libraries) is not guaranteed through the Internet.

There are a few initiatives taking place in different spheres to ensure that the public enjoys further access to knowledge. Leading examples are the previously mentioned open source software, content and standards initiatives. As these initiatives become more widely known to both the public and content and software creators they should be able to expect stronger support. The more important policy question is whether policy makers and institutional managers in local, national and international arenas will be able to recognise and promote the benefits of open knowledge sharing and to establish adequate legal frameworks and practices for ensuring this sharing, in particular for developing countries.

Bibliography

Balser, E. "Teacher Candidate Assessment through Electronic Portfolio Development". *Society for Information Technology and Teacher Education, Albuquerque, NM, Association for the Advancement of Computing in Education*; 2003.

Barclay, D. A. "Teaching Electronic Information Literacy: A How-to-do-it Manual". New York: Neal-Shuman, 1995.

Barnett, D. "Research It! Write It! A Step by Step Guide to Research and Writing". Highsmith Press, 1997.

Bleakley, A., & Carrigan, J. "Resource-Based Learning Activities: Information Literacy for High School Students". Chicago, IL: American Library Association, 1994.

Conan, M. & Heavers, K. "What You Need to Know About Developing Study Skills, Taking Notes and Tests, Using Dictionaries and Libraries". Lincolnwood, IL: National Textbook Company, 1994.

Geier, C. "Electronic Portfolio Assessment in Teacher Education". *Society for Information Technology and Teacher Education, Nashville, TN, Association for the Advancement of Computing in Education*; 2002.

Herner, L. M., S. Karayan, et al. "Special Education Teacher Preparation and the Electronic Portfolio". *Journal of Special Education Technology*. 2003.

Ianuzzi, P. *Teaching Information Literacy Skills*. Boston: Allyn and Bacon, 1998.

Johnson, J. M. "Teacher's portfolio". *Learning and Leading with Technology*. 2000.

Lucena, C., N. Zambrana, et al. "The Electronic Portfolio, a Tool for Reflection in Action and the Transformation of the Student Teacher". *Society for Information Technology and Teacher Education, Albuquerque, NM, Association for the Advancement of Computing in Education*; 2003.

Rose, A. "The Good, The Bad, & The Ugly: lessons learned from electronic portfolio implementation". *Society for Information Technology and Teacher Education, Nashville, TN, Association for the Advancement of Computing in Education*. 2002.

Testerman, J. K. "The electronic portfolio: a means of preparing leaders for application of technology in education". *Educational Administration Abstracts*. 2002.

Walsh, P. and G. Devanney. "Collect, Select and Reflect: Using the Electronic Portfolio in Teacher Preparation". *Society for Information Technology and Teacher Education, Nashville, TN, Association for the Advancement of Computing in Education*; 2002.

Index